MAINE REMEMBERS THOSE WHO SERVED

Tributes from the Pine Tree State

Secretary of State
Dan A. Gwadosky

State of Maine

ISBN 0-9715684-0-5

Maine Remembers Those Who Served was originally printed by J.S. McCarthy/ Letter Systems Printers in 2001.

Copyright © 2001 by the Maine Department of the Secretary of State

MAINE REMEMBERS THOSE WHO SERVED

TRIBUTES FROM THE PINE TREE STATE

TABLE OF CONTENTS

Preface vii

Message from Maine Secretary of State Dan A. Gwadosky ix

Chapter 1   **The Early Wars: Historic Heroes** 1

       Revolutionary War (1775-1783) 3
       War of 1812 (1812-1815) 7
       Civil War (1861-1865) 9
       Spanish-American War (1898) 23

Chapter 2   **The World Wars: Sacrifices Around the Globe** 27

       World War I: "The Great War" (1914-1918) 29
       World War II: (1939-1945) 39
           Background 39
           Pacific Theater of Operations 43
           European Theater of Operations 67

Chapter 3   **The Cold War Era: 1945-1990** 107

       Korean Conflict (1950-1953) 109
       Vietnam Conflict (1961-1975) 123
       International Incidents 145
           Bay of Pigs Invasion (1961) 145
           Cuban Missile Crisis (1962) 147
           Berlin Wall (1969-1970) 150
           Grenada (1983) 152
           Lebanon (1983) 153
           Panama (1988) 155
       Maintaining Peace and Stability 157

Chapter 4 Today: The World's Peacekeepers **161**

    The Persian Gulf War (1990-1991) **163**
    Somalia (1992-1994) **169**
    Haiti (1994) **170**
    Kosovo (1999-present) **171**

Chapter 5 Lifetimes of Service: Careers and Families **173**

    Career Military **175**
    The Sacrifices of Families **181**

Epilogue **191**

Acknowledgements **193**

Maine Medal of Honor Recipients **195**

Appendix **197**

PREFACE

Maine Secretary of State Dan A. Gwadosky, in cooperation with the Maine Veterans' Coordinating Committee, sponsored a new initiative to "promote the vote" for the November 7, 2000 General Election -- the **Vote In Honor of a Veteran** program.

The program provided citizens with the opportunity to go to the polls wearing a button that stated **"I'm Voting in Honor of a Veteran..."** The button was personalized with the name of a veteran that the voter wanted to honor for his or her service to our country and for the sacrifices the veteran made to ensure our important freedoms of self-governance, including the right to vote.

The response to the program was overwhelming. Over 10,000 Maine citizens took advantage of this opportunity to honor someone who had served, or is serving, in the military. Maine voters proudly paid tribute to a grandfather or grandmother, father or mother, brother or sister, son or daughter, husband or wife, or a neighbor, friend or fellow veteran.

From all parts of Maine and 10 other states, the responses honored the service of veterans from the Revolutionary War to the Persian Gulf and Kosovo, from world wars to peacekeeping missions. These tributes, covering a 250-year period, chronicle the contributions of servicemen and women in all branches of the military, celebrate their selfless dedication and commitment to military service, and honor the legacy of their defense of democracy during war as well as peacetime.

This collection, representing just some of the requests to **Vote in Honor of a Veteran**, is a way to show appreciation for all who have served in the military and have helped preserve our right to vote.

It is our way to say "thank you."

To request a button honoring a veteran of your choice, please call the Office of the Secretary of State at (207)626-8400 or e-mail us at *sos.office@state.me.us*.

Message from Maine Secretary of State Dan A. Gwadosky

The response to our **Vote in Honor of a Veteran** project dramatically exceeded our expectations. As we processed the requests, we were moved by the tributes that were provided in response to our simple inquiry, "Please tell us something about the person you are honoring." It seemed only fitting to make some of these stories available to the public.

I am pleased to share this book with you and grateful to the respondents who gave their permission to reprint their tributes and who shared their photographs. I believe you will be as touched by their recollections as I am.

As you will see, citizens took this opportunity to pay tribute to the lives and service of military personnel, most of whom were family members – grandfathers and grandmothers, fathers and mothers, husbands and wives, brothers and sisters, sons and daughters. Others honored friends, historic heroes, and service-related buddies.

Like many of the voters who requested buttons, I wore mine to honor a veteran of World War II, my father, **Joseph Gwadosky**.

He served as a Sergeant in Company C of the 216th Armored Engineering Battalion in the European Theater. Two days after the war ended, he wrote his mother a postcard from Czechoslovakia that said, "Boy, it's good to be coming home for good."

Sgt. Joseph Gwadosky (kneeling on right)

As we assembled this collection, we smiled, we sighed, we cried, and I believe you will too. Many veterans were participants in major world events, and you will find, as I did, that their experiences will enlighten and inspire you. These tributes unite us as a community and prompt us to reflect on the meaning of citizenship, the privilege of voting, and the precious joy of freedom.

Dan A. Gwadosky
Maine Secretary of State

DEDICATION

This book is dedicated to our veterans and their families, whose courage, sacrifice, and honor inspire us all and guarantee that our precious freedoms, including the right to vote, will endure.

Chapter 1

THE EARLY WARS: HISTORIC HEROES

The Revolutionary War (1775-1783)

"The essential principles of our Government...form the bright constellation which has gone before us and guided our steps through an age of revolution and reformation. The wisdom of our sages and blood of our heroes have been devoted to their attainment. They should be the creed of our political faith, the text of civic instruction, the touchstone by which to try the services of those we trust; and should we wander from them in moments of error or of alarm, let us hasten to retrace our steps and to regain the road which alone leads to peace, liberty, and safety."

President Thomas Jefferson (1743-1826)
3rd President of the United States
First Inaugural Address, 1801

Thomas Jefferson, third President of the United States and author of the Declaration of Independence, is perhaps best remembered as a champion of representative democracy and the rights of individuals. These ideals motivated the colonists to fight to be free and independent from British control.

American colonists realized that true separation from the oversight of England would not be achieved without fighting for their rights as free and independent citizens.

At dawn on April 19, 1775, about 70 armed Massachusetts militiamen stand face to face on Lexington Green with the British advance guard. An unordered "shot heard around the world" begins the American Revolution.

A volley of British rifle fire followed by a charge with bayonets leaves eight Americans dead and ten wounded. The British regroup and head for the depot in Concord, destroying the colonists' weapons and supplies. At the **North Bridge in Concord**, a British platoon is attacked by militiamen, with 14 casualties.

I will be voting in honor of my great-great-great-great-grandfather, Captain Isaac Davis, who was a Minuteman in Acton, Massachusetts. He was the first officer killed at the battle of the <u>North Bridge in Concord, Massachusetts.</u>

Joan Cross-Steward, Skowhegan

June 17, 1775 – The first major fight between British and American troops occurs in Boston at the **Battle of Bunker Hill**. American troops are dug in along the high ground of Breed's Hill (the actual location) and are attacked by a frontal assault of over 2,000 British soldiers who storm up the hill. The Americans are ordered not to fire until they can see "the whites of their eyes."

As they get within 15 paces, the Americans let loose a deadly volley of rifle fire and halt the British advance.

The British then regroup and attack 30 minutes later with the same result. A third attack, however, succeeds as the Americans run out of ammunition and are left only with bayonets and stones to defend themselves. The British succeed in taking the hill, but at a loss of half their force, over a thousand casualties, with the Americans losing about 400, including the important colonial leader, General Joseph Warren.

I am voting in honor of Benjamin King, who fought at the <u>Battle of Bunker Hill</u> during the Revolutionary War.

John K. Willard, Gardiner
Served in Korea

Maine's Role in the Revolutionary War

At the time of the American Revolution, Maine, not a State until 1820, was part of Massachusetts. Because of Maine's remoteness from the authorities in Boston and the Continental Congress in Philadelphia, the inhabitants received little military support despite the proximity of the British across the border in Canada and constant pressure from the Royal Navy along the coast. Apart from Benedict Arnold's ill-fated expedition to Quebec through the wilderness of western Maine, most military action took place up and down the vulnerable coast.

June 1775 – A Machias seaman, Jeremiah O'Brien, leads the rebel raid on the British schooner *HMS Margaretta* and two other vessels on the Machias River, the first naval battle of the American Revolution.

The British retaliate by burning the Town of Falmouth (now the City of Portland) in the autumn of that year. Other attempts by Revolutionary forces, like the unsuccessful "Penobscot Expedition" aimed at driving the British out of their fortifications at Castine, also fail. The War for American Independence was successfully fought and won elsewhere.

There were two ways in which a man might serve the Revolutionary cause: most men, like Daniel Sullivan, joined a local militia unit to serve for a three- or nine-month stint, subject to a call-up in response to a nearby emergency; others joined what was known as the Regular Continental Army for three years or for the duration of hostilities. These men were often stationed far from their homes. Their units operated under the direct command of General George Washington.

Several Maine responses, like the following, honored ancestors and early settlers who had served in the Revolutionary War:

> **I am voting in memory of Daniel Sullivan, who was a Revolutionary War hero; our town is named for him. He was Captain of the 2nd Company, 6th Lincoln County Regiment of Militia.**
>
> *Lynn A. Dunbar, Sullivan*

Last Name	First	Middle Init.	Address	Serial No.
Sullivan	Captain Daniel		Sorrento (Hancock Co) Maine	

Date of Birth	At		War
1738	Berwick, Maine	Cause	Revolutionary

Date of Death	At	Cause

Date of Burial	Cemetery	Section No.	Lot No.
	Sorrento	B	1

Grave No.	Book No.	Page No.	Next of Kin
1			

Date of Enlistment	At	Date of Discharge	Branch of Service
July 11, 1776		Sept. 28, 1779	Army

Rank	Type of Marker or Stone
Captain	Upright stone.

War Record
6th
5th Company/Lincoln County Regt.
Additional Comments
Col. Benjamin Foster's Regiment – Captain Company of Volunteers 1779
Service at Machias and Majorbagaduce
Sources: Mass. S & S of Rev. Vol. 15, Page 246

*Grave Registration Card for **Captain Daniel Sullivan**, who served with Colonel Benjamin Foster at Machias and at "Majorbagaduce," now the Town of Castine.*
—Maine State Archives

> **I am voting in honor of Joshua Williams, my 5th great-grandfather by marriage. He served in the Revolutionary War and later founded the Town of Great Pond around 1810.**
>
> *Joan P. Archer, Aurora*

July 10, 1779 – Naval ships from Massachusetts are destroyed by the British while attempting to take the Loyalist stronghold of **Castine**, Maine.

Nathaniel Warren, my great-great-great-great-great-grandfather, served from 1778-1781 in Colonel Henry Jackson's 16th Massachusetts Regiment…He made a forced march from Providence to Boston to relieve the militia on the <u>Castine Expedition</u>.

Charles H. Warren, Scarborough
Served in WWII

When we vote, we will do so in honor of Captain Nathan Daggett, our 5th great-grandfather, who was a captain in the American Revolution.

Lynda N. Quinn, Skowhegan
Vanessa L. Quinn, Skowhegan

Faneuil Hall, Boston (1789)

The War of 1812
America's "Second War for Independence" (1812-1815)

On **June 18, 1812**, the United States declares war on Great Britain after long-standing disputes with the British. For nearly 10 years British ship captains had been impressing American sailors to serve on British ships. Also, Americans are killed and wounded when the British ship *Leopard* fires on the *USS Chesapeake* in 1807 after the Americans refuse to be boarded. In the Northwest Territories Great Britain continues its disputes with the United States at the border with Canada. President Jefferson's attempt to reduce the controversy with the British by introducing the Embargo Act creates an economic disaster for merchants.

In **1808** James Madison is elected President and is re-elected in **1812**. He is pressured by the "War Hawks" in Congress to declare war on Great Britain. The war is labeled "Mr. Madison's War" by the Federalists who oppose it.

By the end of **1812** the British successfully capture Detroit, blockade South Carolina and Georgia, and blockade the Chesapeake and Delaware Bays. By the end of **1813** the British blockade extends to all southern and mid-Atlantic states. By spring of **1814**, the British blockade extends to New England.

Campaigns are waged in the South, the East and the North, with the British undertaking a three-part invasion of the United States at Chesapeake Bay, Lake Champlain, and the mouth of the Mississippi River.

At the Battle of Baltimore, **September 13-14, 1814**, Francis Scott Key writes *"The Star Spangled Banner."*

Fort McHenry

On **February 17, 1815**, the war ends when the Treaty of Ghent is accepted by both the United States and Britain.

The Maine Connection to the War of 1812

At the time of the War of 1812, the District of Maine was still a part of Massachusetts. There are no comprehensive records to indicate how many Maine natives served in the conflict, but undoubtedly many seamen from the District were impressed by the Royal Navy before and after the start of the War. A few individuals, like Joseph Treat of Bangor, served with the regular U. S. Army. He was a captain in the 21st Infantry and participated in heavy fighting in upper New York State and around the Great Lakes. The majority of men were called up by their local militia units, but remained in Maine and saw very little, if any, action.

The Embargo and other trade restrictions profoundly affected Mainers, dependent as they were upon the sea for most manufactured goods coming into the District as well as the export of their principal products, lumber and fish. All sorts of goods became scarce and inflation rose to unprecedented levels. Many merchants had been opposed to Jefferson's Embargo and had initially opposed the War, but by 1813 were resigned to its prosecution. Accordingly, there was a brief surge of joy and hope when, on September 5, 1813, residents along the coast witnessed (or at least heard the gunfire from) a tremendous fight between the British brig *Boxer* and the American brig *Enterprise*. This classic naval battle raged back and forth between Monhegan Island and the mainland and resulted in an American victory.

The seizure by the British of the entire coast east of Penobscot Bay further deepened the economic hardships of the residents of Maine. The Massachusetts Legislature refused to take any action to relieve or defend Maine and instead improved their own fortifications. President Madison then nationalized the Maine militia, placing it under the command of William King, a local militia Major General. But the Federal Government had no funds to support, arm, or equip the locals, who had to continue to endure the British occupation. There were countless unpleasant incidents, some crops and stores were burned or destroyed, but fortunately, the British seldom carried out such threats as that issued by a Captain Barry to the citizens of Hampden: "My business is to burn, sink and destroy. Your town is taken by storm, and by the rules of war, we ought both to lay your village in ashes, and put its inhabitants to the sword. But I will spare your lives, though I mean to burn your houses." It should be noted, however, that one reason the British were reluctant to harm the inhabitants of the occupied area was that they claimed the entire region as part of Canada and did not want to inflame residents who, according to them, were by rights British subjects. The actual boundary between Maine and Canada was not settled until 1842.

The most important result of the War of 1812 upon the citizens of Maine was that it fanned the movement for independence from Massachusetts. This had been a growing issue before the war, but the utter failure of Massachusetts to assist the District of Maine in any way brought the matter to a head. William King, who had been in charge of the Maine Militia, became the principal leader of the drive for statehood. Joseph Treat, who had served in the Western theater of the War, was a member of several conventions leading up to the signing of the Constitution of Maine, and upon achieving statehood in 1820, William King was elected the first governor of the State of Maine.

Material taken from William D. Williamson, ***The History of Maine from Its First Discovery, A. D. 1602 to The Separation, A. D. 1820, Inclusive.*** Hallowell, 1832, and selected records in Maine State Archives

The Civil War (1861-1865)

"...Now we are engaged in a great civil war, testing whether that nation or any nation so conceived and so dedicated can long endure. We are met on a great battlefield of that war. We have come to dedicate a portion of that field as a final resting-place for those who here gave their lives that that nation might live. It is altogether fitting and proper that we should do this..."

Abraham Lincoln (1809-1865)
16th President of the United States
The Gettysburg Address
November 19, 1863

September 17, 1862 – This date marks the bloodiest day in U.S. military history as General Robert E. Lee and the Confederate Armies are stopped at **Antietam** in Maryland by General George B. McClellan and numerically superior Union forces. By nightfall an estimated 23,000 men are dead and wounded. Lee withdraws to Virginia.

I am voting in honor of my great-grandfather, Wilson C. Fitzgerald. He fought with Company F, 7th Maine Infantry Regiment at the Siege of Yorktown, the Battle of Williamsburg, the engagement at Mechanicsville, the Battle of Fair Oaks, the Battles of Savage Station, White Oak Swamp and Malvern Hill, the engagement at South Mountain and the <u>Battle of Antietam</u>.

(My uncle, named after my great-grandfather, served in the Army during WWII in the Battle of the Bulge.)

Mark C. Fitzgerald, Bath
Served during Vietnam era

December 13, 1862 – The Army of the Potomac under General Burnside suffers a costly defeat at **Fredericksburg**, Virginia, with a loss of 12,653 men after 14 frontal assaults on well-entrenched Rebels on Marye's Heights. "We might as well have tried to take hell," a Union soldier remarks. Confederate losses are 5,309.

"It is well that war is so terrible – we should grow too fond of it," stated Lee during the fighting.

I am honoring my great uncle, Jerome R. Hodge, who served in the Union Army during the Civil War. He was killed at the <u>Battle of Fredricksburg</u> on December 12, 1862. He gave his life so that others could be free.

James R. Hodge, Arundel
Served in Korea

July 1-3, 1863 – The tide of war turns against the South, as the Confederates are defeated at the **Battle of Gettysburg** in Pennsylvania. During three hot summer days, what began as a skirmish ended in the most famous and most important battle of the war, involving more than 160,000 Americans. Confederate casualties in dead, wounded and missing were 28,000 out of 75,000 soldiers. Union casualties were 23,000 out of 88,000.

Aaron Adams (my great-great uncle) was a private in H Company, 20th Maine Regiment at <u>Gettysburg</u>. He was a 27-year-old farmer from Linneus, Maine, and he was killed at Little Round Top. He died so all men might be free. Aaron was never married and town records indicate he owned a horse when he left for Gettysburg to defend freedom and justice.

Gena Pelletier, Durham

*Summary service record card for **Aaron Adams**, Company H, 20th Maine Infantry, killed at **Gettysburg**, July 2, 1863* —Maine State Archives

*Composite copy of the original casualty report of the 20th Maine at **Gettysburg**. **Aaron Adams'** name is third from the top. The entire list shows a total of 129 men killed, wounded or captured.*
—Maine State Archives

When I vote, I will pay tribute to my great-grandfather Henry Hartshorn, who fought at <u>Gettysburg</u>. He was in the 19th Maine Regiment. He got wounded in the knee, got gangrene, and came home to Belfast where he died in 1889.

Elizabeth Nibby, Morrill

John Thomas Smith, my great-great-grandfather, served with Company G, 20th Maine Infantry, 1861-65. He was shot in the shoulder July 2 at <u>Gettysburg</u> and taken prisoner, spent 6 months in Libby Prison, and mustered out with his unit in April, 1865.

Larry R. Smith, Wiscasset
Served in Vietnam era

*Summary service record card of **John T. Smith**, Company G, 20th Maine Infantry.*
—*Maine State Archives*

June 15, 1864 – Union forces miss an opportunity to capture **Petersburg**, Virginia and cut off the Confederate rail lines. As a result, a nine-month siege of **Petersburg** begins with Grant's forces surrounding Lee.

My great-great-great-great-grandfather, James Alden Grant, served in the War of the Republic in Company B, 7th Maine Infantry, as a private. He died at Petersburg, on June 18, 1864.

Chester E. Nichols, Jr., Harrington
Served in US Coast Guard for over 20 years

John Ervin, my great-great-grandfather, was a Corporal in Company I, 32nd Maine Regiment. He was wounded at Petersburg June, 1864, in the shoulder and mustered out December 12, 1864.

George E. Spulick, Alfred
Served during Korean Conflict

I am voting in honor of my grandfather, George P. Derenburger. He joined the Union Army in August, 1862 with the 11th West Virginia Volunteers. He was wounded at the Battle of Snickers Ferry and a second time at the Battle of Petersburg. He was discharged in June 1865.

Patrick L. Derenburger, Oxford
Served 21 years in US Navy, including Vietnam

I am voting in honor of my great-grandfather, Horatio A. Thurston, who enlisted when he was just 18 years old, and his brother, Stephen D. Thurston, who enlisted at age 36. They mustered in on December 26, 1863 and served in the 1st Maine Regiment, Company G, Heavy Artillery. Stephen was wounded in the thigh on June 18, 1864, at the <u>Battle of Petersburg</u>.

H. Richard Norton, China

In the **summer of 1864**, a handful of Confederate agents crossed the border from New Brunswick, Canada, and robbed a bank in Calais, Maine. In the same period, Confederate raiders sailed secretly into Portland Harbor and stole the U.S. Revenue Cutter *Caleb Cushing* from under the noses of the authorities. Little harm was done as a result of these incidents, but coastal inhabitants felt themselves under constant threat.

Three men honored in this chapter – *Fields Baston, Sylvester King* and *John Towle* – served with the 1st Maine Heavy Artillery. This unit spent most of the War manning fortifications around Washington, D.C., but in the spring of 1864 General Ulysses S. Grant pulled them out of Washington and reassigned them to combat duty in Virginia alongside the infantry. They were thrown into some of the bloodiest fighting of the entire War. In the space of 10 months, at Petersburg alone, 66.5 percent of their unit strength became casualties.

February 1864 - April 1865 – Andersonville Prison (Georgia) was a military stockade of the Confederate army used to confine captured Union army enlisted men. A total of 49,485 prisoners were detained at Andersonville. As many as 30,000 men were confined there at one time. More than 13,700 prisoners died in confinement. Constant exposure to the elements, together with inadequate food, impure water, congestion, and filth, led inevitably to epidemics of scurvy and dysentery.

Andersonville Prison

Oscar Thomas served in the Union Army during the Civil War and was a prisoner of war at <u>Andersonville</u>.

Dalton E. Neal, Lincoln
Served in Korea

Oscar Thomas

*Summary service record card for **Oscar Thomas**, Company I, 20th Maine Infantry. He originally enlisted in Company K, 2nd Maine Infantry and was subsequently transferred to the 20th.*
—Maine State Archives

Nahum Davis

I will be voting in honor of Nahum Davis, my great grandfather, who served as a private in the Civil War. He was wounded and taken to <u>Andersonville Prison</u>. He died there from abusive treatment and starvation. He received a posthumous citation from Joshua Chamberlain in 1868.

Philip N. Martin, Sullivan

*Joshua L. Chamberlain is best remembered for two great events: the **action** at Little Round Top on the second day of Gettysburg (July 2, 1863), when then-colonel Chamberlain and the 20th Maine held the extreme left flank of the Union line against a fierce rebel attack, and the **surrender** of Lee's Army of Northern Virginia at Appomattox, when Grant chose Chamberlain to receive the formal surrender of weapons and colors (April 12, 1865). Always a chivalrous man, Chamberlain had his men salute the defeated Confederates as they marched by, evidence of his admiration of their valor and of Grant's wish to encourage the rebel armies still in the field to accept the peace.*

Joshua Chamberlain
—NARA photo

On Election Day, I will be voting in honor of Joshua L. Chamberlain.

Richard Stearns, Thomaston
Served in Vietnam

In recent years, the 20th Maine, commanded by Joshua Chamberlain, has garnered immense publicity, somewhat to the detriment of other units. For example, few now know of the stand of the 19th Maine (represented by honored veteran Henry Hartshorn), who withstood some of the worst of Pickett's Charge at Gettysburg on July 3, 1863. Hardly anyone knows of the suffering of those units who were sent to Florida, Louisiana, and Mississippi, where disease took a far greater toll than did combat. In just nine months, they lost 11 men in combat, while 143 members of the regiment died of disease.

> During the Civil War, a **regiment** was the basic unit in the organizational structure, both North and South. Each **regiment** was made up of 10 **companies** consisting of 100 men each, making each regiment a unit of 1,000 men, plus an additional 10-12 field officers.
> A **brigade** consisted of 3, or occasionally 4, regiments.
> A **division** consisted of 3 to 4 brigades.
> A **corps** included 3 to 4 divisions.
> An **army** was comprised of a varied number of corps, i.e. Army of the Potomac, Army of the Cumberland, Army of Northern Virginia.
>
> Thus, the 20th Maine looked like this in full:
> **20th Maine Volunteer Infantry, 3rd Brigade, 1st Division, 5th Corps, Army of the Potomac.**
>
> —*Maine State Archives*

> "Allow me to thank you for your letter – hearty and affectionate beyond the custom of epistles of condolence or congratulation, even among friends. I assure you I place this among my treasures and trophies – kept for my children – & not the least (if you will permit me) among the "laurels" of which you so kindly speak.
>
> ...I long to be in the field again, doing my part to keep the old flag up, with all its stars.
>
> Your friend & servant
> J.L. Chamberlain"

Chamberlain was so severely wounded on June 18, 1864, that he was not expected to live. He did survive, however, and went on to become Governor of Maine for four successive terms, and President of Bowdoin College for many years. Ultimately, he did die of complications arising from his wounds, but not until 1914. Here is part of a letter he wrote to the Adjutant General of Maine while he was recuperating in a hospital at Annapolis, Maryland in the summer of 1864.
—Maine State Archives

It is said that Maine contributed one of the largest percentages of troops for the Union cause of any state, in proportion to the available manpower it had to offer. Some 70,000 Mainers fought in the State's volunteer units, in the Regular U.S. Army, or with units from other states, while some 5,000 seamen served in the navy. On its own, Maine raised 32 regiments of infantry, 2 regiments of cavalry, 1 regiment of heavy artillery, 1 regiment of light (mounted) artillery, 1 company of sharpshooters, 20 companies of unassigned infantry who either remained in Maine or were incorporated into existing regiments, and several companies of coast guard and coast guard artillery who protected Maine's vulnerable coastline.

Of the dozens of other Maine voters who honored veterans of the Civil War, many proudly recalled relatives who had served in a number of different Maine units:

Our great-grandfather, Porter S. Knight of Waterboro, served in the 127th Maine Regiment*, Company K, in defense of Washington, D.C.

Erlane C. Sargent, Buxton
Bernard J. Knight, Buxton
Served in WWII
Kenneth E. Knight, Buxton

**This likely was the 27th Maine*

In 1864, at age 43, my great-grandfather, Sylvester R. King, enlisted in the Union Army. He served with Company L, 1st Maine Artillery. He was discharged on June 14, 1865, and died May 5, 1912.

Ellsworth W. Smith, Lincoln
Served in the South Pacific during WWII

*Summary service record card for **Sylvester King**, Company L, 1st Maine Heavy Artillery. King was one of three veterans honored in this collection who were in the 1st Maine Heavy Artillery.* —Maine State Archives

I am voting in honor of my great-grandfather George B. Lyon (1844-1927). He was a member of the 31st Maine Infantry Division in the Civil War and was wounded seriously in the latter part of the war and reportedly carried the rifle slug the rest of his life.

Phillip E. Butler, Carmel
Served in WWII

John R. Towle

My great-grandfather, John R. Towle, enlisted on August 21, 1862 in the 1st Maine Artillery. He was wounded in the leg and discharged in 1865.

Joyce Austin, Dexter

*Summary service record for **John R. Towle**, Company A, 20th Maine Infantry, one of three veterans honored in this collection who were in the 1st Maine Heavy Artillery.*
—*Maine State Archives*

I will be voting in honor of my great-grandfather, John S. Davis, who served in Company H of the 17th Maine in the War Between the States.

John E. Usher, Sr., Hollis
Served in the Navy during Vietnam

Among responses remembering Civil War veterans were also those that honored relatives who had served with the Confederate forces:

My great-uncle, John J. MacKey, served with the North Carolina Cavalry during the Civil War. He was from Buncombe County. He did not surrender – he walked home.

Christopher D. Chamberlin, Parsonsfield
Served in Vietnam, 1969-70

My great-grandfather, Daniel Crosby, fought in the War Between the States in the 9th Regiment of the South Carolina Infantry. He died from wounds in battles at Swift Creek, Virginia in 1864.

Charles Harvey Warren, Scarborough
Served in WWII

> Despite lack of historic evidence, local veterans groups honor the grave of the Unknown Confederate Soldier in Durham's Strout Cemetery, and they do so because he was a Civil War soldier and an American veteran.
>
> There are several stories about how a Confederate soldier could have ended up in Maine. According to one account, "A Durham (Maine) couple found a man in a gray Confederate uniform in the casket that was supposed to contain the body of their son. Unsure of where they should send the casket, they buried the man in the corner of Strout Cemetery." In another tale, "the fallen Confederate was mistakenly sent to Maine instead of Durham, North Carolina." A third version suggests that "the soldier died on his way to Canada following his escape from a New York prison."
>
> —*Associated Press, April 17, 2001*

Other Mainers honored relatives who proudly served during the War Between the States:

My great-great-grandfather Jonathan Carter was wounded in the left shoulder at <u>Port Hudson, Louisiana</u>, in the Civil War.

Dale Carter, Presque Isle
Served in US Air Force, 1958-79

*Summary service record for **Jonathan Carter**, Company E, 28th Maine Infantry, wounded severely before <u>Port Hudson, Louisiana</u>, June 22, 1863.* —Maine State Archives

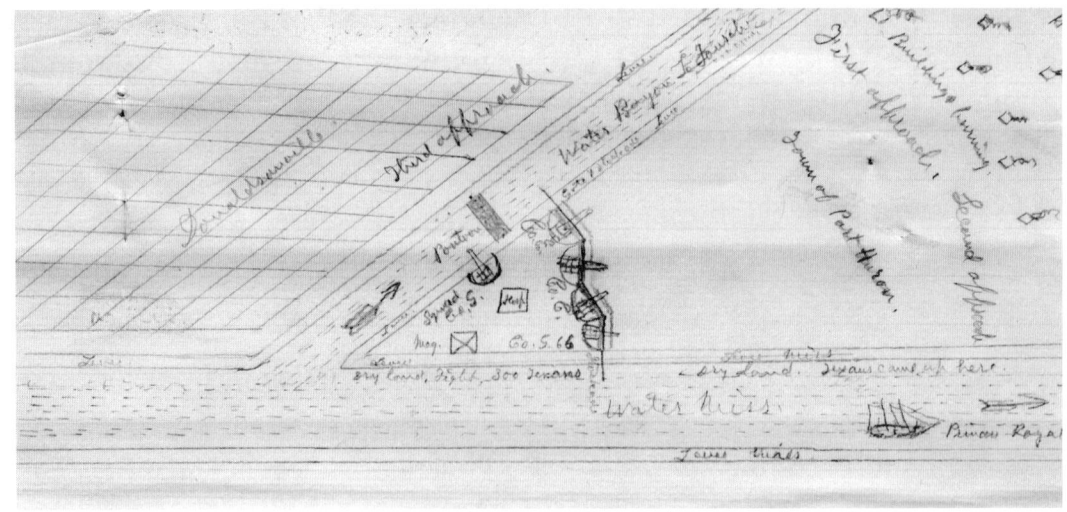

Drawing by Captain Augustine Thompson of the 28th Maine shows fortifications around <u>Port Hudson, Louisiana</u>. —Maine State Archives

I am proud to vote in honor of Garret Dedrick, Jr., my great-great-grandfather, who served with the 161st Infantry, New York, during the War of the States. He was born on January 25, 1827, and raised in Sidney, Delaware County, New York. At the age of 35, Garret enlisted and was mustered in the 161st New York Infantry, Company G in Binghamton, New York. He served the Union Army until April 18, 1864, when he was discharged at New Orleans due to heart disease. In 1872 he moved his family westward to Smith Center, Kansas, and homesteaded there until spring of 1886. In February 1890 he died of "La Grippe" in Colby, Kansas.

Monica McCusker, Lisbon

John Nicholas Ackerman, my great-grandfather, served in the 22nd Regiment, Company K in Indiana.*

Doris A. Merry, Bucksport

**This probably was Company K, 22nd Indiana Infantry.*

I will be voting in honor of my grandfather, Leonard Oscar White, who was in the 5th Massachusetts in the Civil War.

Lois W. Young, Swanville

Leonard Oscar White

Cpl. Fields Baston, my great-uncle (by marriage), was a soldier in the Union Army in the Civil War. He was killed in action May 19, 1864 in the Battle for the Spottsylvania Courthouse in Virginia while replacing an American flag which had been torn down by Confederate forces.

Evarts T. Leighton, Bangor

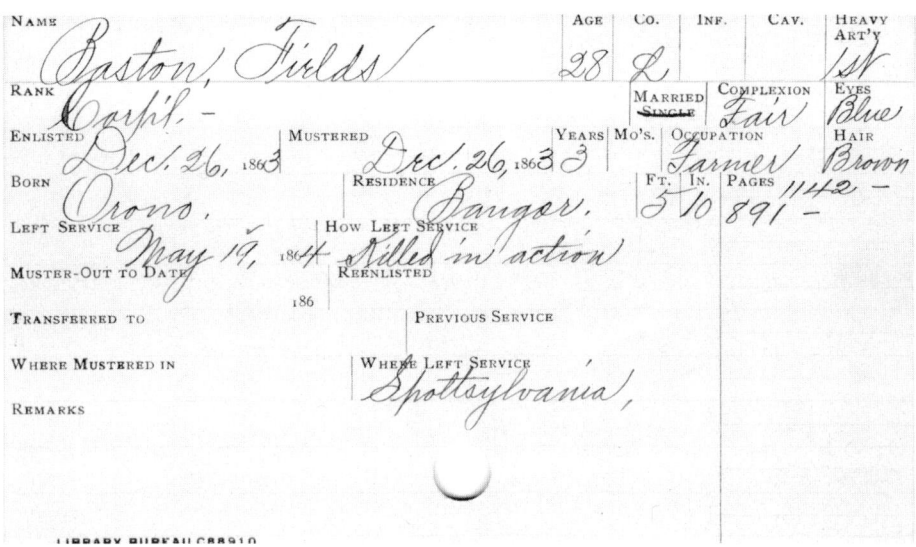

*Summary service record card for **Fields Baston**, Company L, 1st Maine Heavy Artillery, killed at Spottsylvania on May 19, 1864. Baston is one of three honored veterans in this chapter who served in the 1st Maine Heavy Artillery.* —Maine State Archives

This is the monument to the 1st Maine Heavy Artillery at Petersburg National Battlefield.

Spottsylvania Battlefield

*The names of the 115 members of the **1st Maine Heavy Artillery** who were killed outright at Petersburg, as well as the 489 men of the regiment who were wounded in the same action, are inscribed on this monument. Of these men, 95 subsequently died. Of the 2,057 units in the Union Army during the Civil War, this regiment sustained the greatest loss in battle.*

April 9, 1865 – Gen. Robert E. Lee surrenders his Confederate Army to Gen. Ulysses S. Grant at Appomattox, Virginia. Grant allows Rebel officers to keep their sidearms and permits soldiers to keep horses and mules.

April 10, 1865 – Celebrations break out in Washington.

April 14, 1865 – President Abraham Lincoln is shot during the 3rd Act of "Our American Cousin" at Ford's Theater. He dies the next morning.

May 1865 – Remaining Confederate troops surrender. The Nation is reunited.

Over 620,000 Americans died in the War Between the States, with disease killing twice as many as those lost in battle. Approximately 50,000 survivors returned home as amputees.

December 6, 1865 – *The Thirteenth Amendment abolishing slavery is ratified.*

The Spanish-American War (1898)

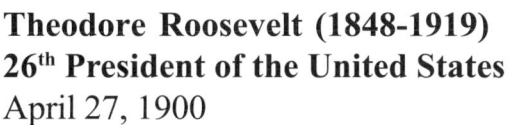

"We meet here to pay glad homage to the memory of our illustrious dead; but let us keep ever clear before our minds the fact that mere lip-loyalty is no loyalty at all, and that the only homage that counts is the homage of deeds, not of words. It is but an idle waste of time to celebrate the memory of the dead unless we, the living, in our lives strive to show ourselves not unworthy of them. If the careers of Washington and Grant are not vital and full of meaning to us, if they are merely part of the storied past, and stir us to no eager emulation in the ceaseless, endless war for right against wrong, then the root of right thinking is not in us, and where we do not think right we cannot act right."

Theodore Roosevelt (1848-1919)
26th President of the United States
April 27, 1900

January 24, 1898 – The *USS Maine* arrives in Havana harbor in Cuba on a "friendly" visit. Three weeks later, on February 15, 1898, the *Maine* is shattered by two separate explosions and rapidly sinks. This incident leaves 254 seamen dead, and 59 sailors wounded. Eight of the wounded later die.

After the disaster, U.S. newspapers are quick to place responsibility for the loss on Spain. A U.S. Navy court of inquiry concludes that the ship was sunk by a mine, but it could not fix responsibility upon any person or persons, including the government or military forces of Spain. (Later studies indicated a possibility that the *Maine* sank as a result of a coal bunker fire adjacent to one of its ammunition magazines.)

However, the loss of the *Maine* turns American popular opinion strongly in favor of war with Spain. Hundreds of editorials demand that the *Maine* and American honor be avenged. Soon the rallying cry is everywhere: "Remember the *Maine*! To hell with Spain."

*The **USS Maine** rested on the floor of Havana Harbor until 1911. Eventually the wreck was recovered and then sunk at sea. She now rests at 3,600 feet. However, many artifacts from the ship were recovered and given to towns, cities and organizations across the country.*

—U.S. Navy photo

*Among the mementos recovered from the **USS Maine** is her bow scroll, now located in Davenport Park on the corner of Main Street and Cedar Street in Bangor, Maine. The scroll was cleaned and refurbished during the centennial and is considered by many to be one of the most remarkable artifacts from the ship.*

*The silver service from the **USS Maine**, on permanent loan from the U.S. Navy, is currently on display in the dining room of the Blaine House in Augusta.*

Recovered by divers after the ship was sunk, the soup tureen and two serving dishes are decorated with pine cones and tassels and the Great Seal of the State of Maine.

Several Maine citizens honored the contributions of military personnel during this period of American engagement abroad:

My grandfather, Albert J. Yager, served on the *USS Kentucky* during the Spanish-American War.

Gail Bogdanski, Sangerville

Horace E. Moore, my grandfather, served in the 1st Maine Artillery in the Spanish-American War.*

John E. Moore, Brewer

*He served in the 1st Battalion, Heavy Artillery, U.S. Army.

Horace E. Moore

*Summary service record card of **Horace E. Moore**, Battery B, 1st Battalion, Heavy Artillery, U.S. Army, Spanish-American War.* —Maine State Archives

I am voting in honor of my grandfather, William Joseph Stephens, who fought in the Spanish-American War. He died in WWI with the Princess Patricia's Canadian Light Infantry in Yerps, France.

Carl H. Smith, Falmouth
Served in Vietnam era

I pay tribute to William Winders, who served in the Spanish-American War. He was over 100 years old when I took care of him as a visiting nurse in Denver, Colorado, over 30 years ago.

Elizabeth F. Wisecup, Windham

Cpl. Harry G. Carey, my grandfather, was born in the Isle of Jersey, England. He came to the U.S. with his family and became a U.S. citizen on October 15, 1890. He "enrolled" in Company M of the 47th Regiment of New York in 1898 for two years or "during the war" and was promoted to rank of Corporal on November 28, 1898 in Caguas, Puerto Rico. He was awarded the New York State Decoration for Service and was "mustered out of the Regiment" on March 31, 1899.

Constance J. Footman, Durham

May 1, 1898 – Commodore George Dewey leads a naval victory in Manila Bay in the Philippines.

May 21, 1898 – U.S. Navy takes control of Guam.

June 29, 1898 – Skirmish between U.S. and Spanish troops near Santiago, Cuba.

July 1, 1898 – Battle of San Juan Hill, Cuba. Teddy Roosevelt and his Rough Riders win notoriety. Roosevelt returns to U.S. a hero.

July 3, 1898 – Spanish fleet destroyed off Santiago Bay, Cuba.

July 25, 1898 – U.S. forces land in Puerto Rico.

August 12-13, 1898 – Spain agrees to armistice.

December 10, 1898 – Treaty of Paris is signed.

Chapter 2

THE WORLD WARS: SACRIFICES AROUND THE GLOBE

World War I: "The Great War" (1914-1918)

"It is a war against all nations. American ships have been sunk, American lives taken, in ways which it has stirred us very deeply to learn of, but the ships and people of other neutral and friendly nations have been sunk and overwhelmed in the waters in the same way. There has been no discrimination. The challenge is to all mankind. Each nation must decide for itself how it will meet it. The choice we make for ourselves must be made with a moderation of counsel and a temperateness of judgment befitting our character and our motives as a nation. We must put excited feelings away. Our motive will not be revenge or the victorious assertion of the physical might of the nation, but only the vindication of right, of human right, of which we are only a single champion."

President Woodrow Wilson (1856-1924)
28th President of the United States
War Message to Congress
April 2, 1917

June 28, 1914 – The assassination of Archduke Ferdinand at Sarajevo sets in motion the diplomatic maneuvers that result in war.

August 1, 1914 – Germany declares war on Russia and on **August 3, 1914**, declares war on France.

War becomes widespread. When Germany violates Belgian neutrality, Great Britain enters the war with the Allied Nations of France, Russia, Serbia, Belgium, and Japan against the Central Powers of Germany and Austria-Hungary.

The war continues. Portugal and Romania join the Allies in **1916**; Greece declares war on the Central Powers in **1917**.

April 6, 1917 – The United States breaks off its relations with Germany and enters the war.

President Wilson delivers War Address to Congress, April 2, 1917.

In **June 1917**, the first troops of the American Expeditionary Forces (AEF), commanded by **General Pershing**, land in **France**.

> **I vote in honor of Allan Picard, who served with General John Pershing against the Mexican bandit Pancho Villa and later was one of the first men from Millinocket to enlist in World War I.**
>
> *John C. Picard, Millinocket*
> *Served in Vietnam*

*The responses about World War I veterans who served in **France** reveal the affection and honor with which they are remembered:*

> **I'll be proud to cast my vote in honor of my friend, Everett McKenney, who served in the Army in France during World War I. In July 1999, he received the Legion of Honor, France's highest award given to foreigners, from the French consul. He died at the age of 104 on September 3, 1999. Although his military service had ended over 80 years earlier, it was still one of the most important, most defining, aspects of his life.**
>
> *Robin Wilkinson, Augusta*

Everett McKenney

I am voting in honor of my father, Grover L. Johnson, who served in the U.S. Army in <u>France</u> in 1918 and received a testimonial attesting to his patriotism, valor and devotion to duty from the State of Maine.

George Robert Johnson, Brunswick
Served in WWII, Korea & Vietnam

My uncle, Sgt. Guy Malcolm Yeaton, served with the 5th Marines, 2nd Division and was killed in action at Blanc Mont Ridge, <u>France</u>, on October 4, 1918, the bloodiest day of the war. 1,000 men had to take Blanc Mont Ridge where the Germans had been entrenched for 4 years. When the battle was over, the Germans were dead or running. There were 134 Marines left standing.

Sgt. Yeaton fought in every major battle in France. He received the highest awards for valor that the French military had to offer, including the Cour de Geir. In letters home – all addressed from "somewhere in France" –the family learned he was recommended for the Distinguished Service Cross. To my knowledge, he never received it because he was killed shortly thereafter.

Guy Malcolm Yeaton

If people like my uncle hadn't fought in WWI, would we be where we are today?

David P. Speed, Isleboro
USCG (Ret.)

Marion MacEwan, my great-aunt, was a Scottish immigrant who enlisted in the U.S. Army Nurse Corps during WWI. She served 10 miles behind the front lines in <u>France</u>. Nurses were ordered to leave the wounded if the Germans invaded, but all nurses refused to obey the order. She is buried at Arlington Cemetery.

Nancy L. Kuzil-Roberts, Windsor
Served in Korea

I will vote in honor of my great-uncle, George McKelvey, who was in the Army stationed in <u>France</u> in World War I. He was thrown in a pile for dead. When he came home, he carried with him his death papers.

George McKelvey

McKelvey's great-niece provided the following unidentified newspaper account:

"*McElvey's outfit, Company L of the 320th Infantry, was making an advance in the Argonne Forest on October 11, 1918, exactly one month before the Armistice. The Germans were beginning to crack up, but they were still putting up a tough defensive battle as they retreated. Everything was going well for George until a German machine-gun sniper ripped him with sixteen slugs while he was trying to dodge across an open clearing.*

From then on, he was unable to walk and totally unable to use his left arm. A corporal with his right wrist shot off carried, rolled, and dragged him to a First Aid Station behind the lines. There was rain, they ploughed through mud, and just before they got there, the Boche laid down a gas barrage. The two of them, with only two usable hands between them, managed to get gas masks adjusted on each other.

McKelvey was then carried to a sector hospital to have some more patching done. The hospital was filled to the gills, and they had to lay him on the soggy ground outside with the other wounded soldiers. Five minutes after his turn came and he was moved into the hospital, a German shrapnel shell burst over the others still remaining in the courtyard.

On February 2, 1920, after staying in hospitals in France and at Camp Meade, McKelvey arrived at his home in Johnetta, Pennsylvania. His family still thought he was dead and had a certificate from the War Department to prove it. They had even conducted funeral services at the family cemetery plot. But it was a gala day for Johnetta after they got over the shock of seeing a dead man walking.

The Overseas Medal and the Order of the Purple Heart were awarded to George. He received them from Washington through the mail after the war."

Elizabeth Pulk, Dixfield

PROJECT HONORS FORGOTTEN SACRIFICES

"On November 30, 1917, a 24-year-old soldier named Harold T. Andrews became the first man from Maine to die in World War I. He was killed while fighting off German soldiers with a shovel on the battlefield in France, far from his Portland home.

His valiant sacrifice was honored in 1921 with a memorial planting of linden trees along Baxter Boulevard that still exists today, even though the public largely is unaware of their symbolism."

—*from the Archives of the **Portland Press Herald**
December 3, 2000*

*Some Maine voters specifically recalled their **fathers'** experiences in this war:*

My father, Paul F. "Ginger" Fraser, served in France and Germany in the First World War as an officer in the infantry. He had to lift his gas mask to issue orders and the mustard gas left him with a damaged heart. He died at age 45 as a result of his heart damage. I will be proud to cast my vote on Election Day in his honor and in honor of all of our veterans.

Janet F. Mitchell, Waterville

Paul F. Fraser

I will be voting in honor of my father, Otto O. Winn, who served in the Army, Company G, 103rd Infantry in the First World War. He was wounded in action and received the Purple Heart and a picture signed by Woodrow Wilson. A parade was held for his homecoming and the local newspaper covered it all.

Linda E. Szostek, Bangor

Otto O. Winn

My father, Ralph O. Stevens, served in WWI. He was gassed in Germany. He died from it 15 years later. I was only 3 years old.

Carolyn Ferguson, Biddeford

Benjamin B. Twitchell, Sr., my father, served in WWI in the 151st Depot Brigade. A horse or mule kicked him while he was hooking up a piece of artillery equipment. Because of this accident, he lost his left eye and had to have a steel plate in his forehead.

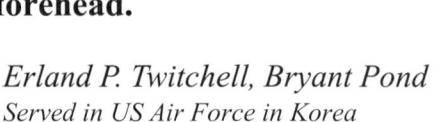

Erland P. Twitchell, Bryant Pond
Served in US Air Force in Korea

Benjamin B. Twitchell, Sr.

I will cast my vote in tribute to my father, Carl R. Young, a WWI veteran. His unit trained at Bates College in Lewiston before going to Europe. After that war, he met many WWII casualties and assisted families with a proper military burial if the family requested his help. He also played a part in the American Legion's work on the GI bill, which produced very important results for veterans. He voted in every election. My mother did also. Voting was especially important to her because she could not legally vote until she was 26 – she was born in 1894.*

William A. Young, Auburn
Served in Korea from 1951-55

*The 19th Amendment to the Constitution, ratified on August 18, 1920, guarantees all American women the right to vote.

I vote in honor of my father, Peter P. Mich, who served in the Army in WWI.

Peter J. Mich, Englewood, FL
Served in the Pacific, 1944-46

I am paying tribute to my father, Morris Shapiro, who joined the Jewish Legion of the British Army in WWI. He served in Palestine and fought against the Turkish Army. He served in the same regiment with Ben-Gurion, future Israeli Prime Minister.

Samuel Shapiro, Waterville
Served in WWII, former Treasurer, State of Maine

Morris Shapiro

Several responses, like the following, included information from veterans' diaries. **Frank J. Mulcahey,** *kept a diary during his service in France. His son, Daniel Mulcahey, shared the following details of his father's travels:*

> **Travel of 79th Division, WWI (1918). Left Camp Meade, Maryland, July 6th. Entrained at Disney, Maryland for port of embarkation, which was Hoboken, New Jersey. Boarded ship USS Leviathan July 7th. Sailed 6:20 p.m., July 8th, arrived at Brest, France 11:00 a.m. July 15th. Hiked to a rest camp 5 miles. Arrived there at 11:00 p.m. Parade at Brest. Left rest camp 2:00 a.m. July 19th. Hiked back to city of Brest for a 3-day ride in box cars (side door Pullmans) to the town Largnes. Left Largnes 8:00 am July 22nd. Hiked 9 miles to Coulmer-Le-Sector. Left Coulmer-Le-Sector July 24th in motor trucks for a 40-mile ride to Pierrecourt (lost on road)… Remained on front line until November 20th.**
>
> *Daniel Mulcahey, Brooks*
> Served in Vietnam

Interesting stories about the ***citizenship*** *of military personnel were the focus for some of the World War I responses:*

> **I am voting in honor of my father, William A. Naimey, who served in the Army in World War I and gained his citizenship through the service.**
>
> *Norman W. Naimey, Cape Elizabeth*
> Served in Korea

> **My grandfather, Wesley Thompson, was an American citizen who fought in the Army for Canada before the U.S. entered WWI. He earned the Victoria Cross but died in action 3 days before the war ended.**
>
> *Wesley B. Thompson, Auburn*

> **My father, Walter Szlyk, came to the United States from Poland. He enlisted in the U.S. Army Air Corps during WWI and served at Kelly Field in Texas.**
>
> *Paul R. Szlyk, D.M.D., York Beach*
> Served in Dental Corps in Greenland &
> Ft. Devens

Walter Szlyk

*In several requests for buttons, writers identified **the job** that a veteran had during his military service:*

I am voting in honor of my grandfather, Robert A. Craig, Sr., who served in Compay C, 301ˢᵗ Ammunition Train, Camp Devens, Massachusetts. He left Mars Hill on April 27, 1918, and after training at Camp Devens, he went by train to Montreal, then down the St. Lawrence to Quebec and on to Halifax. His convoy sailed from there to Liverpool, England, and then on to Cherbourg, France. During his military service he drove a Harley with a sidecar that carried officers to the front lines.

Robert A. Craig, Sr.

This picture of him was taken in a French war studio in Noyers, France at a cost of twelve francs for one dozen pictures.
Army pay at the time was $33.00 a month with $6.50 deducted for insurance, leaving him with a net wage of $26.50! After his service, he went on to earn his living repairing jewelry and clocks in southern and central Aroostook.

Stuart Craig, Mars Hill
Served in US Navy, 1976-79

My father, Frank Lumbert, was stationed in Massachusetts during WWI and on his discharge papers it states that he was saddler.

Lillian Mabel Adams, Canton

*Equally interesting were responses that made special mention of a veteran's **age**:*

My grandfather, Maurice LeBlanc, served in WWI and was used as an interpreter. He joined at age 42 – he lied about his age and ended up going to France with his son.

Maurice A. White, Castle Hill
Served in Vietnam

My great-uncle, Donald F. Crain, is a WWI vet. He's still alive at 102!!

Daniel Hawes, Steep Falls

The War Ends

At 11:00 a.m. on November 11, 1918, World War I ended – and the Armistice was signed. Germany had to evacuate its troops immediately from all territory west of the Rhine. The war ended without a single truly decisive battle having been fought.

To calculate the total losses caused by the war is impossible. A conservative estimate is about 10 million dead and 20 million wounded. Because this immense suffering gave rise to a general revulsion to any kind of war, many people placed their hopes for peace in the newly created League of Nations.

Regrettably, World War I, the "war to end all wars," represented a transition to a new kind of warfare, one that harnessed the power of air forces, chemical weapons, mechanized artillery and tanks – all of which laid the groundwork for the Second World War.

In 1919, President Woodrow Wilson proclaimed November 11th as Armistice Day to remind Americans of the tragedies of war. A law adopted in 1938 made the day a federal holiday.

In 1954, Congress changed the name of the holiday to Veterans Day to honor all veterans.

—U.S. Navy image

The following poem by John J. McCrae remains one of the most memorable war poems ever written. It recalls a terrible battle in the spring of 1915. Major McCrae was a surgeon attached to the 1ˢᵗ Field Artillery Brigade who had spent 17 days treating injured men – Canadians, British, Indians, French, and Germans. The death of a young friend and former student on May 2, 1915 so affected him that he composed this now-famous poem.

IN FLANDERS FIELDS

In Flanders fields the poppies blow
Between the crosses, row on row,
That mark our place; and in the sky
The larks, still bravely singing, fly
Scarce heard amid the guns below.

We are the Dead. Short days ago
We lived, felt dawn, saw sunset glow,
Loved, and were loved, and now we lie.
In Flanders fields.

Take up our quarrel with the foe:
To you from failing hands we throw
The torch; be yours to hold it high.
If ye break faith with us who die
We shall not sleep, though poppies grow
In Flanders fields.

World War II (1939-1945)

The U.S. Entry into the Second World War

Wars

In the old wars drum of hoofs and the beat of shod feet.
In the new wars hum of motors and the tread of rubber tires.
In the wars to come silent wheels and whirr of rods not yet dreamed out in the heads of men.

In the old wars clutches of short swords and jabs into faces with spears.
In the new wars long range guns and smashed walls, guns running a spit of metal and men falling in tens and twenties.
In the wars to come new silent deaths, new silent hurlers not yet dreamed out in the heads of men.

In the old wars kings quarreling and thousands of men following.
In the new wars kings quarreling and millions of men following.
In the wars to come kings kicked under the dust and millions of men following great causes not yet dreamed out in the heads of men.

from **War Poems**
by **Carl Sandburg**
American poet, 1878-1967

Axis Powers Invade Europe

September 1, 1939 – World War II begins when Germany, without a declaration of war, invades Poland. Britain and France declare war on Germany on September 3, 1939. All the members of the Commonwealth of Nations, except Ireland, follow suit.

Spring, 1940 – Germany invades Denmark and Norway. German troops overrun Luxembourg, invade the Netherlands and Belgium and drive their armored columns to the English Channel. Great Britain resists the German attempt to bomb it into submission, but it is the only Allied power remaining.

June 22, 1941 – Germany invades the Soviet Union and destroys much of European Russia. However, the harsh winter curtails the German sweep to Moscow. Great Britain and the Soviet Union become allies.

The United States Enters the War

Initially, the United States' biggest concern is to protect commercial ships from attacks by German submarines.

The United States formally protests the aggressive acts of Japan in China, Indochina, and Thailand.

Despite attempts to maintain its neutrality, the United States enters the world conflict.

December 7, 1941 – Without warning, Japan attacks Pearl Harbor.

The twisted remains of the destroyer USS Shaw burning in floating dry dock at Pearl Harbor after the "sneak Japanese attack" on Dec. 7, 1941.

Early in the morning of Sunday, December 7, 1941, carrier-based planes of the Japanese Imperial Navy conduct a surprise attack on the United States Naval Base at Pearl Harbor. Approximately 100 ships – battleships, destroyers, cruisers, and support ships – are in the harbor that morning. The rest of the Pacific fleet is out to sea. Nearby Hickam Air Field is also attacked by the Japanese planes.

In the raid eight American battleships and 13 other naval vessels are sunk or badly damaged. The *USS Arizona* is completely destroyed and the *USS Oklahoma* capsized. More than 180 aircraft are destroyed.

Approximately 2,400 military personnel are killed.

A hurried dispatch from the ranking United States naval officer in Pearl Harbor provides the first official word of the attack: "Air Raid on Pearl Harbor. This is not a drill."

On December 8, 1941, President Franklin D. Roosevelt addresses the Congress of the United States. In this brief six-minute speech President Roosevelt delivers what some have regarded as the most famous phrase uttered by an American President: "Yesterday, December 7, 1941 – a date which will live in infamy – the United States of America was suddenly and deliberately attacked by naval and air forces of the Empire of Japan."

*Maine ties to **Pearl Harbor** bring the war home:*

I am voting in honor of my brother, Sumner A. Sessions, who served 32 years in the Air Force. He was a <u>Pearl Harbor</u> survivor, having been at Hickam Air Field on December 7. His military career included service in WWII, Korea, and Vietnam.

Robert E. Sessions, Norway
Served in WWII, Battle of the Bulge

I want to pay tribute to my husband, Louis R. Mathieson, who joined the Navy in May 1940. He was on the *USS Oklahoma* at <u>Pearl Harbor</u> at the time of the attack. He has been a good husband for 56 years and is the father of 5, grandfather of 10, and great-grandfather of 5.

Vera Payson Mathieson, Owl's Head

Louis R. Mathieson

I am voting in honor of my grandfather, John Chase. He was too old for the draft but after hearing the radio announcement about <u>Pearl Harbor</u>, he immediately signed up. He served in the Army and went into Japan after the nuclear devastation.

Andrew Roth-Wells, Georgetown

Joseph E. Cyr, my husband, was a <u>Pearl Harbor</u> survivor. He served in the military for 5 years. He died November 20, 1999 at the age of 80. We had been married 52 years and 3 months and we have 2 daughters.

Theresa L. Cyr, Saco

I am voting in honor of my husband Patrick W. Murphy, who served 21 years in the Navy, retiring as a Chief Petty Officer. He was at <u>Pearl Harbor</u> on December 7, 1941, on the *USS Vestal* at anchor by the *USS Arizona*.

Carmen F. Murphy, Sanford
Served in WWII and Korea

Patrick W. Murphy

The entire text of **President Roosevelt's speech** follows:

Yesterday, December 7, 1941 – a date which will live in infamy – the United States of America was suddenly and deliberately attacked by naval and air forces of the Empire of Japan.

The United States was at peace with that nation and, at the solicitation of Japan, was still in conversation with the government and its emperor looking toward the maintenance of peace in the Pacific.

Indeed, one hour after Japanese air squadrons had commenced bombing in Oahu, the Japanese Ambassador to the United States and his colleagues delivered to the Secretary of State a formal reply to a recent American message. While this reply stated that it seemed useless to continue the existing diplomatic negotiations, it contained no threat or hint of war or armed attack.

It will be recorded that the distance of Hawaii from Japan makes it obvious that the attack was deliberately planned many days or even weeks ago. During the intervening time, the Japanese government has deliberately sought to deceive the United States by false statements and expressions of hope for continued peace.

The attack yesterday on the Hawaiian islands has caused severe damage to American naval and military forces. Very many American lives have been lost. In addition, American ships have been reported on the high seas between San Francisco and Honolulu.

Yesterday, the Japanese government also launched an attack against Malaya.

Last night, Japanese forces attacked Hong Kong.

Last night, Japanese forces attacked Guam.

Last night, Japanese forces attacked the Philippine Islands.

Last night, the Japanese attacked Wake Island.

This morning, the Japanese attacked Midway Island.

Japan has, therefore, undertaken a surprise offensive extending throughout the Pacific area. The facts of yesterday speak for themselves. The people of the United States have already formed their opinions and well understand the implications to the very life and safety of our nation.

As commander in chief of the Army and Navy, I have directed that all measures be taken for our defense.

Always will we remember the character of the onslaught against us. No matter how long it may take us to overcome this premeditated invasion, the American people in their righteous might will win through to absolute victory.

I believe I interpret the will of the Congress and of the people when I assert that we will not only defend ourselves to the uttermost, but will make very certain that this form of treachery shall never endanger us again.

Hostilities exist. There is no blinking at the fact that our people, our territory and our interests are in grave danger.

With confidence in our armed forces – with unbounding determination of our people – we will gain the inevitable triumph – so help us God.

I ask that the Congress declare that since the unprovoked and dastardly attack by Japan on Sunday, December 7, a state of war has existed between the United States and the Japanese Empire."

President Franklin D. Roosevelt
Pearl Harbor Speech to Congress
December 8, 1941

The Pacific Theater of Operations (1941-1945)

"And when at some future date the high court of history sits in judgment on each one of us – recording whether in our brief span of service we fulfilled our responsibilities to the state – our success or failure, in whatever office we may hold, will be measured by the answers to four questions: were we truly men of courage...were we truly men of judgment...were we truly men of integrity...were we truly men of dedication?"

John Fitzgerald Kennedy (1917-1963)
35th President of the United States
Address to a Joint Convention of the General Court of the Commonwealth of Massachusetts, January 9, 1961

—U.S. Bureau of Engraving photo

Japanese Empire at its Height

December 1941 – After bombing Pearl Harbor, Japan continues its aggression in the Pacific, invading the Philippines and Guam on December 10, 1941, Burma on December 11, British Borneo on December 16, Hong Kong on December 18, and Luzon in the Philippines on December 22. They take Wake Island on December 23, 1941. General Douglas MacArthur begins the U.S. withdrawal from Manila in the Philippines to Bataan. On December 27, 1941, the Japanese bomb Manila.

January 1942 – Japan captures Manila and the U.S. Naval base at Cavite on January 2, attacks Bataan in the Philippines on January 7, invades Dutch East Indies and Dutch Borneo on January 11, and advances into Burma on January 16. On January 27, 1942, the first Japanese warship is sunk by a U.S. submarine.

February 1942 – U.S. involvement in the Pacific increases. On February 1, the first aircraft carriers, *Yorktown* and *Enterprise*, conduct air raids on Japanese bases in the Gilbert and Marshall Islands. On February 24, the *Enterprise* attacks the Japanese on Wake Island. However, the Japanese continue their offensive actions, invading Java in the Dutch East Indies, Singapore, Sumatra, Bali and Darwin, Australia.

On February 22, President Roosevelt orders General MacArthur out of the Philippines. The largest U.S. warship in the Far East, the *Houston*, is sunk.

March 1942 – Action in the South Pacific continues to escalate. The British evacuate Rangoon in Burma; the Dutch surrender on Java. Japan invades the Andaman Islands in the Bay of Bengal. On March 11, General MacArthur leaves Corregidor for Australia. President Roosevelt appoints him commander of the Southwest Pacific Theater.

Here is an interesting Maine connection to General MacArthur:

I am voting in honor of my father, Reverend Edwin T. Cooke, who served from 1939-1945 as Chief of Chaplains in the South Pacific on General Douglas MacArthur's staff.

Dwight H. Cooke, Rockland
Served in WW II and Korea

Edwin T. Cooke

On March 24, Admiral Chester Nimitz is appointed Commander in Chief of the U.S. Pacific Theater.

April 1942 – Outnumbered and short of food and medical supplies, American and Filipino soldiers hold out for three months defending Luzon on the Bataan Peninsula. Malaria, dysentery, and tropical diseases are rampant. On April 3, the Japanese attack the troops at Bataan. Six days later the U.S. forces on Bataan surrender unconditionally to the Japanese. On April 10, the **Bataan Death March** begins.

Estimates of the number of American and Filipino prisoners who started the march vary widely. There were probably 76,000 Allied POW's, including 12,000 Americans, forced to walk 60 miles under a blazing sun without food or water toward a new POW camp, resulting in over 5,000 American deaths from malnutrition, disease and atrocious treatment by their captors.

*Mainers recall veterans who endured the **Bataan Death March**:*

I will be voting in honor of my brother, Pvt. Hugh P. Parsons, who served in the Army, Ground Air Corps. He was stationed in the Philippines, taken prisoner by the Japanese, survived the <u>Bataan Death March</u>, but died of dysentery in a POW camp on Luzon on September 23, 1942.

He and his two cousins, Charles Baird and Arthur Calderwood, and their close friend, Harold Morrison, had grown up together on North Haven and enlisted in the Army together in 1940. All four survived the Bataan Death March but all four died while POWs in the Pacific Theater. We, as a family, and the community as a whole lost, sacrificed, four wonderful young men.

Hugh P. Parsons

Betty P. Brown, North Haven

When I vote, I will do so in tribute to Stanley B. Durgin. He enlisted in the Army Air Corps in early 1941 and was sent to the Philippines in November. His plane was diverted by the attack at Pearl Harbor. His bomb group was formed into a Provisional Infantry Battalion. The Japanese pushed Americans down the Bataan peninsula. Durgin was wounded in the fighting. He was taken prisoner but survived the Bataan Death March. He was incarcerated in Japan for more than 3 years. His POW camp was within the primary target of the second atomic bomb, but weather conditions forced the drop on the secondary target, Nagasaki.

Stanley B. Durgin - 1945

This is a copy of the identification card made by the Japanese for Stanley B. Durgin (Picture taken in 1942 in Japanese prison camp)

James W. Taylor, Jr., South Paris
Served in WW II, European Theater

May 1942 – The action continues. The Japanese occupy Mandalay in Burma, take Tulagi in the Solomon Islands, and prepare to invade Midway and the Aleutian Islands. They take **Corregidor** when General Wainwright unconditionally surrenders all U.S. and Filippino forces in the Philippines.

I will be voting in honor of the 503d ABN Infantry Regiment. They jumped on Corregidor in the Second World War.

SFC Albert B. Heimann, Machias
Member of 503d ABN Inf Reg from 1955-1964
US Army (Ret.)

I am remembering my friend Evan Thurlow. He died in a Japanese prison camp after being captured in Corregidor.

Lester O. Delano, Lee
Served in WWII

June 4-5, 1942 – A turning point in the war occurs at the Battle of Midway. Squadrons of U.S. torpedo planes and bombers from the *Enterprise*, *Hornet,* and *Yorktown* attack and destroy four Japanese carriers and a cruiser, and damage another cruiser and two destroyers. The U.S. loses the *Yorktown*.

Patricia McNally

I am voting in honor of my aunt, Patricia (Cox) McNally, who served stateside during WWII.

According to a local newspaper account provided by her niece, *Patricia McNally joined SPARs, "Semper Paratus-Always Ready," the women's backup to the Coast Guard during WWII. "She spoke wistfully of how the ships, carrying Coast Guardsmen off to the Pacific – off to war – would slip out silently in the night without warning."*

Kerry M. Cox, Bangor
Served in Vietnam

August 7, 1942 – The 1st Marine Division invades Tulagi and **Guadalcanal** in the Solomon Islands. It is the first U.S. amphibious landing of the war. A day later eight Japanese warships retaliate and sink three U.S. heavy cruisers, an Australian cruiser, and one U.S. destroyer, in less than an hour. Over 1,500 Allied crewmen are lost. Nearly two weeks later, on August 21, 1942, U.S. Marines repulse the first major Japanese ground attack on **Guadalcanal**, setting the stage for the Battle of Bloody Ridge on Guadalcanal from September 12-14, 1942.

Family members voted on Election Day in honor of Joseph P. Anastasio, who served in the South Pacific; they sent a copy of his "Enlisted Record and Report of Honorable Discharge" indicating that he had served in <u>Guadalcanal</u>, the North Solomons, New Guinea, and Luzon during his tour of duty from March 17, 1941 to August 15, 1945. And, according to these records, he received $300 "mustering out pay."

Elaine Anastasio (wife), Rumford
Jo-Ann Anastasio (daughter), Augusta
David Anastasio (son), Rumford

I am voting in honor of my friend, Phil Collins, Staff Sgt, who was in the U.S. Marines for 16 years. He was in major battles including Guadalcanal, Cape Glaster, and Peleiu. He was wounded on Peleiu and was one of seven of the entire company to survive. He received a letter of commendation and 7 battle medals.

Philip J. Theriault, Augusta
Served in Korea

Phil Collins

October - November 1942 – Heavy fighting continues. In October, U.S. cruisers and destroyers defeat a Japanese task force off **Guadalcanal**. The first U.S. Army troops, the 164th Infantry Regiment, land on Guadalcanal. In November, U.S. and Japanese warships clash again off **Guadalcanal**, resulting in the sinking of *USS Juneau* and the highly publicized loss of the five Sullivan brothers.

The **Sullivan family** lived in Waterloo, Iowa, a town of about 50,000 people. When they learned that a friend had died on the *USS Arizona* during the attack on Pearl Harbor, the five brothers – George, Frank, Joseph, Madison, and Albert – decided to enlist in the Navy. They insisted on staying together throughout their service despite an official Navy policy of separating brothers. Eleven months later, on November 13, 1942, they were crew members on the *USS Juneau* when a Japanese submarine sunk the ship. All five brothers perished, and a nation joined a family in mourning the loss of the "fighting Sullivan brothers."

I am voting in honor of my father, John J. Kaiser, Sr., a career Navy Chief Petty Officer, who gave his life during the Battle of Savo Island during World War II. The *USS Juneau* was sunk by Japanese naval forces during a night attack at Guadalcanal.

John J. Kaiser, Jr., Brunswick
Served in Korea and Vietnam

December 31, 1942 – Emperor Hirohito of Japan gives permission to his troops to withdraw from Guadalcanal after five months of bloody fighting against U.S. forces. However, they do not begin their evacuation for over a month.

January 1943 – The Allies succeed in overpowering Japanese troops in New Guinea.

February 9, 1943 – The Japanese resistance on Guadalcanal finally ends.

April 18, 1943 – U.S. code breakers identify the location of Japanese Admiral Yamamoto near Bougainville in the Solomon Islands.

Lydia Truc Franz

My adopted mother, Lydia Truc Franz, was a sergeant in the Women's Army Corps. She was a crypt-analyst during WWII stationed at Arlington Hall, Virginia, deciphering Japanese code. She memorized 500 4-digit numbers and then scanned the code, which had been intercepted, to identify letters. She was on duty when the bombs were dropped. After the war she was sent to Shang Hai, China, as part of the Occupation Army.

Kathleen Ross, Owl's Head

I am voting in honor of my mom, Sophia Burnell, and my dad, Ernest Burnell. Both of them served during WWII in the Pacific Theater working in Army Intelligence/Radio Encryption.

Ernest J. Burnell, North Sebago
Served in Vietnam

July 8, 1943 – B-24 Liberators flying from Midway bomb the Japanese on Wake Island.

August 1 and 2, 1943 – 15 U.S. PT-boats attempt to block Japanese convoys in the Solomon Islands. PT-109, commanded by Lieutenant John F. Kennedy, is rammed and sunk by a Japanese cruiser, killing two. The remaining crew survive, but some are severely injured. Kennedy heroically aids a badly injured sailor.

John F. Kennedy in PT-109
—navygames.com photo

August - December 1943 – The fighting intensifies. The Allies complete the occupation of New Georgia and recapture New Guinea. U.S. Marines invade the Solomon Islands. Emperor Hirohito states his country's situation is now "truly grave."

Mainers remember heroic sacrifices from veterans during this period:

My first cousin, Normand Dostie, was an aerial gunner in the Army Air Force. He was K.I.A. ("Killed in Action") October of 1943 over Leyte Island in the Philippines during World War II. He never came back to us. His headstone was placed just last year at the Maine Veterans Memorial Cemetery in the "Garden of Remembrance" with 18 others from Maine who never came back.

Emile La Chance, Augusta
Served in Korea, 1951-52

I am voting in honor of my husband, Roland "Bud" Finley.

As described in a November 9, 2000 article* in the **Moosehead Messenger** provided by his wife, *Staff Sergeant Finley served in the South Pacific and was the only survivor of a Japanese bombing attack that killed the 14 other soldiers "hunkered down on an island one mile long and one-half mile wide, close to the island of New Guinea." Finley received shrapnel wounds but returned to his post, waited for the bomber to return, and downed the Japanese plane on its fourth swing over the airstrip. For these actions he received the Purple Heart.*

Roland & Eunice Finley

Roland Finley

Eunice Finley, Dover-Foxcroft

*According to the same article, the Finleys take care of 1,150 veterans' graves, including those who served in the Revolutionary War.

49

I am proud to vote in honor of Junior N. Van Noy, "a 19-year-old American boy who gave his all for his country on battle-scarred Scarlet Beach in New Guinea, far from his beloved Idaho."

For his heroism, Van Noy received the Medal of Honor.

CITATION

"The Medal of Honor citation is awarded to Pvt. Junior N. Van Noy for gallantry and intrepidity above and beyond the call of duty in action with the enemy near Finschhafen, New Guinea, on 17 October 1943. He was gunner in charge of a machine-gun post only five yards from the water's edge when the alarm was given that three enemy barges loaded with troops were approaching the beach in the early morning darkness. One landing barge was sunk by Allied fire, but the other two beached ten yards from Private Van Noy's emplacement. Despite his exposed position, he poured a withering hail of fire into the debarking enemy troops. His loader was wounded by a grenade and evacuated. Private Van Noy, also grievously wounded, remained at his post, ignoring calls of nearby soldiers urging him to withdraw, and continued alone to fire with deadly accuracy. He expended every round and was found covered with wounds, dead beside his gun. In this action, Private Van Noy killed at least half of the thirty-nine enemy taking part in the landing. His heroic tenacity at the price of his life not only saved the lives of many of his comrades but enabled them to annihilate the attacking detachment."

Franklin J. Martin, Bangor
Served in New Guinea,
Philippines & Bismarck Archipelago

January - October 1944 – Allies make headway in the Pacific Theater. U.S. troops capture the Marshall Islands, attack the Mariana Islands, invade New Guinea, and bomb railways in Thailand. U.S. Marines invade Guam and Tinian. The U.S. conducts air raids against Okinawa. A decisive U.S. Naval victory occurs at Leyte in the **Philippines**.

Mainers pay tribute to gallantry and sacrifice in the Pacific Theater:

I am voting in honor of my cousin, 1st Lt. Roland Albert, who was a navigator on a B-29 bomber lost over China in 1944 or 1945. Years later the remains of all the crew were buried at Arlington Cemetery.

Lionel E. Pelletier, Lewiston

My great-uncle, Merton Bridges, was in many major battles in WWII (Leyte, Okinawa, etc.) The last year of his life he finally talked about his experiences.

Molly T. Varnum, Sedgwick

My uncle, Dominic DeFilipp, just passed away at the age of 83. He had received a Purple Heart for wounds he received in the <u>Philippines</u>. He was the son of Italian immigrants who upheld the American dream even though he was fighting against those of his native tongue. He was a good man who deserves to be honored.

Christina DeFilipp, Kennebunkport

I am proud of my father, Charles I. Pentland. He was a Captain who served in parts of the U.S. and Japan. He is 79 years old now.

Priscilla D. Hoekstra, Etna

I am voting in honor of my father, Lt. M. Dewing Proctor, who was strafed while stationed on Mindoro Island in the <u>Philippines</u>. It was Christmas Eve 1944 and his men were playing cards. He went out to check the refueling tanks so they could finish their game. He died the next day. In his letters home to my mother he wrote often about why he was there and how he wanted his baby daughter (me) to grow up in a free country. My mother learned how to be a single parent, and neighbors and relatives filled in all the empty spots in my life, as so many Americans did for those left behind. Voting in my father's name, serving in public life, and respecting the government he fought to save for me are the ways I honor both his sacrifice and the gifts others gave to me and to my mother.

Mrs. Marion Proctor and daughter Anne (Proctor) Larrivee accept Lt. Proctor's Bronze Star.

Anne Larrivee, New Gloucester

The Western Union telegram reads as follows:

"THE SECRETARY OF WAR ASKS THAT I ASSURE YOU OF HIS DEEP SYMPATHY IN THE LOSS OF YOUR HUSBAND SECOND LIEUTENANT MORRIS D PROCTOR REPORT RECEIVED STATES HE DIED TWENTY FIVE DECEMBER ON MINDORO AS RESULT OF WOUNDS RECEIVED IN ACTION CONFIRMING LETTER FOLLOWS. DUNLOP ACTING THE ADJUTANT GENERAL."

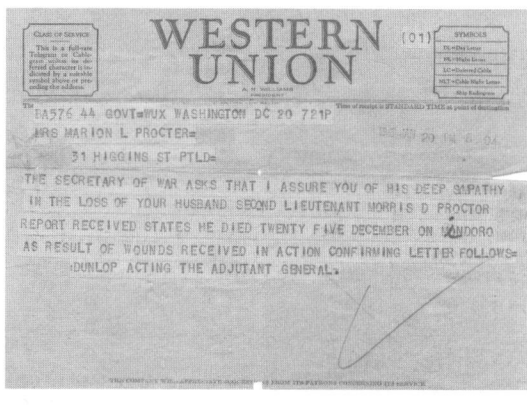

Marion Proctor carried this telegram from the Secretary of War in her purse until her death in 1999.

My father, Merle S. Tilton, Sr., was a sergeant in the USMC and served 5 years during WWII on "recon" patrol in the South Pacific (the Marshall Islands, the Gilbert Islands, Okinawa). For 15 years he was Company Commander for the Maine Army National Guard at the Waterville Armory.

After 20 years he retired as a Captain in the Maine Army National Guard. I am very proud of my father and what he sacrificed during the horrors of war. I can't even imagine what he went through.

Jeffrey Troy Tilton, Richmond
Served in Desert Storm, currently stationed at Brunswick Naval Air Station

Merle S. Tilton, Sr.

My husband, Durward W. Carroll, was one of three brothers who served in three different services in World War II: Army/Air Force, Navy, and Army. My husband served in Guam and Okinawa. His father had to sign for him to enlist – he was only 17 years old. He had a chance to stay stateside but chose not to.

Jane B. Carroll, Lincoln

Durward W. Carroll

Mary Adams Patterson's story is representative of the extraordinary contributions of many women who, like the men of their time, left home and family to serve their country and then returned to Maine to resume their lives, raise their families, and serve their communities.

Several loved ones, including Tami Patterson and Patrick Patterson of Garland, wrote to praise the contributions of Mary Eileen Adams Patterson, R.N. According to family accounts, she served from 1944-47 as an active duty nurse, including service in the Pacific Theater. After the war ended, she was assigned to inactive duty and in 1951 was honorably discharged from the Navy to return home to Maine.

I am voting in honor of my mother, Mary A. Patterson, who graduated from Eastern Maine General Hospital in Bangor in 1943. She was the oldest of Mr. and Mrs. George Clarence Adams' 14 children from East Holden, Maine.

Rita M. Hall, Brewer

My grandmother, Mary A. Patterson, boarded a train in Bangor and waved goodbye to a crying mother, a very emotional mother because Mary's brother, William C. Adams, was in Europe with the Army, and another brother, John E. Adams, would join her soon for basic training at Sampson, NY. Her father was away working at the South Portland Shipyard and Mary's sister Pauline joined the Cadet Nurse Corps.

Aaron Markey, Carmel

My mother, Mary Patterson, told her stories to us as children and she didn't sugar coat them. She told about combat, death, suffering, and sacrifice on the part of our military and the struggles of being a woman veteran.

Claire P. Winchester, Bangor

Mary Adams Patterson

When I vote, I will honor my oldest sister, Mary Adams Patterson, who volunteered for duty wherever necessary. She was sent to Guam and Saipan. We never saved any of her interesting letters, but I do remember her telling us that, after talking with natives and missionaries on Saipan, Mary believed Amelia Earhart died there.

George C. Adams, East Holden

"Kamikaze" attacks were raids conducted during World War II by Japanese pilots who had been trained to make suicidal crashes with airplanes often loaded with explosives.

October 25, 1944 – The first suicide air attacks – the notorious "kamikaze" attacks – occur against U.S. warships in Leyte Gulf. By the end of the war, Japan will have sent 2,257 aircraft on these missions.

Paul J. Yenco, my husband, is deceased as of 1990. During World War II, he was in the Navy and piloted the smaller boats from the large ships, bringing the troops to land. He joined the Navy on December 28, 1942 and was discharged on January 23, 1946. He told me of the many Japanese suicide planes that were constantly over their ship and many nearly hit. He told me after we were married in 1954, that he was prepared to die for he thought he'd never live through it all, but he thanked his mom for her constant prayers.

Paul J. Yenco

His ship finally came back to California to prepare for a big invasion to Japan but thank God victory was declared and he came home. The only wound he had was a cut on his left arm from a Japanese soldier who had stabbed him when he was returning with a boatload of troops to the main ship. Apparently no one noticed the soldier had a knife. He was a prisoner and attacked Paul in the boat. Otherwise, you could say he was lucky for he was always in "the thick of it"–his quote.

Addie M. Yenco, Lisbon Falls

December 17, 1944 – The U.S. Air Force begins preparations for dropping the atomic bomb by organizing the 509th Composite Group to operate the B-29's that will deliver the bomb.

January 3, 1945 – General MacArthur is placed in command of all U.S. ground forces and Admiral Nimitz is put in command of all naval forces in preparation for planned assaults against **Iwo Jima**, **Okinawa**, and **Japan** itself.

I am voting in honor of the 22nd Marines Reinforced FMF (Fleet Marine Force*), who fought in <u>Okinawa</u> in 1945. They liberated the capitol of Okinawa and were awarded the Presidential Unit Citation.

*Fleet Marine Force includes ground and air units designed to serve with the fleet for seizing and defending advanced naval bases and for conducting such land operations as may be essential in the prosecution of a naval campaign.

The following account is taken from an article written by Tom Bartlett for *Leatherneck* magazine, December 1976:

"On May 10, the Sixth Marine Division was ready to lead the Allied drive toward Naha, the Okinawa capitol. The 22nd Regiment would pave the way, with its 2nd Battalion maintaining contact with the First Marine Division and the 3rd Battalion on the seacoast.

Marine engineers did the impossible; Marine tanks did the incredible; individual efforts by Marine grunts, officers and corpsmen overcame all obstacles, whether manmade or natural.

And when it was over, 75,000 Japanese were killed; 10,755 (mostly Okinawa and Korean Conscripts) were captured. American losses were also heavy; 7,373 killed. 31,807 wounded and 239 missing.

It was 101 days from start to finish of the Okinawa campaign when the bulk of the Sixth Marine Division embarked and withdrew to Guam.

The Sixth Marine Division had never seen the United States throughout its 19 months of existence. Formed overseas, the division's members fought overseas. They also disbanded overseas.

Combat decorations were presented. A total of 1,592 Sixth Marine Division members stepped forward to receive awards from their division commander."

Louis J. Batas, Old Town
Served in WWII and Korea

Lt. Millard H. Patten Jr. was my best friend. He served in the U.S. Marine Corps and was killed in the <u>Battle of Okinawa</u>.

According to Patten's obituary included in Mr. Treworgy's tribute, *"About 500 yards from camp they came across an area showing signs of Japanese activity. Lt. Patten took two enlisted men and went off to investigate a small ravine to one flank…There were several small cave openings in the ravine, one of which appeared to have been recently occupied. One of the men started forward to look into the cave, but Lt. Patten stopped him and said he would go first. As he bent over to look into the cave, a Japanese soldier inside shot and instantly killed him, the bullet entering the base of his skull. The two men with Lt. Patten immediately engaged in a fierce close range fight with the Japanese in the cave in order to retrieve his body, which they did…In all, six Japanese soldiers were killed and a large stock of demolition charges captured but at the irreplaceable cost of the lives of two excellent young American officers."*

Millard H. Patten, Jr.

Carl L. Treworgy, Hallowell

January – February 1945 – U.S. military activity heightens. The Sixth Army invades **Luzon** in the Philippines and attacks the Japanese in Manila.

My uncle, James A. Ferguson, was the remaining son of 3 boys in the Ferguson family, and he gave his life for his country in the Second World War on Luzon.

Roland C. Ferguson, Biddeford
Served in Korea

*The following tribute represents the deep **friendships** that develop through shared military experiences:*

Captain John A. Titcomb, USMC, was from a well-to-do family in Farmington; he went to Texas A & M, was married and had small children. I was from a poor farm family in Damariscotta Mills and only had attended high school. We both trained in close air support. We first met in Luzon, the Philippines in late January 1945. We were involved in the battle for Manila and to free the 3,500+ inmates of Santo Tomas Internment Camp. On March 1, 1945, Captain Titcomb was killed by a Japanese sniper's bullet while directing a close air support mission from the front lines. Marine Captain John A. Titcomb – officer, gentleman, husband, father, and friend – was a credit to the Corps and a very brave fighting Marine.

Phillip E. Armstrong, South Portland
Served in the Pacific in the early 1940's

February 19 - March 16, 1945 – U.S. Marines invade and capture **Iwo Jima**.

Flag raising on Iwo Jima. February 23, 1945.

I will vote in tribute to John Bradley, who died in January 1994, and was the last surviving Navy Corpsman from the group of 6 Marines who raised the flag on Iwo Jima.

Robert O. Brown, South Portland
Served in Korea and Vietnam

Alcee A. Vigue
(1944)

My husband, Alcee A. Vigue, served in the Navy in WWII on the *USS Hyman* in the South Pacific in Iwo Jima and Okinawa. He was hit by a kamikaze attack and saw the raising of the flag on Mount Suribachi on Iwo Jima.

Mrs. Cecile M. Vigue, Fairfield

Alcee A. Vigue
(2001)

I will be voting in honor of my friend, Lt. John Holt. We served together in the 483rd Battalion in the Pacific Islands operations.

Attached to Mr. Johnson's tribute are Lt. Holt's memoirs, including the following recollections:

"Remember hiding in bushes on Ulithi watching the naval officers and Admirals Halsey and Nimitz dancing with the nurses? Remember washing clothes on Iwo with homemade propeller-driven washing machines? Remember heating coffee over steaming holes in the ground and heating water in helmets on an old 90mm shell stuck in the steam hole? Remember ever seeing a piece of green grass or bush or anything but volcanic ash on Iwo? (I don't.)"

Lt. John Holt, Sgt. Harold Johnson
Btry "B" 483rd AAA

Harold J. Johnson, South Portland
Served on Pacific Islands of Anguar, Ulithi, and Iwo Jima

I am voting in honor of Louie Paré. He served with the Marines on Iwo Jima in WWII and earned a Purple Heart. He later served with the U.S. Army as a surveyor in the Philippines.

Alan S. Grover, Monroe
Served as a U.S. Navy Photographer, including work in aerial mapping and surveillance

In 36 days of the fiercest fighting of World War II, three divisions of the U.S. Marine Corps captured the island of Iwo Jima. More than 60,000 Americans fought on Iwo Jima. At the end of the battle, 6,821 Americans lay dead. An additional 21,865 Americans suffered wounds or combat fatigue.

April 1, 1945 – The final amphibious landing of the war occurs as the Tenth Army invades Okinawa. By June 22, 1945, they complete their capture of Okinawa when Japanese resistance ends.

April 12, 1945 – President Roosevelt dies and is succeeded by Vice President Harry S. Truman.

President Harry S. Truman
33rd President of the United States

U.S. Intensifies its Assault on Japan

April - July 1945 – U.S. intensifies its assault of Japanese on land, in the air, and on the sea. B-29s fly their first fighter-escorted mission against Japan with P-51 Mustangs based on Iwo Jima. By mid-July 1,000 bomber raids against Japan begin.

Joseph Gardiner Currier

I am voting in honor of my brother, 1ˢᵗ Lt. Joseph Gardiner Currier, who was a bombardier on a B-29. He was shot down on a mission over Kawaski, Japan, on April 16, 1945. He was taken prisoner and declared dead one year later. His personal belongings never came back.

Mary Loyola Albert, Bangor

Our dad, Earl J. St. Laurence, was a B-29 pilot and proud of it. He quit high school to join the Army Air Force. He flew bombing and weather reconnaissance missions from North Field in Guam to Japan. He was forced down on Iwo because of a gas leak and was chased by the Japanese coming out of the jungle on take off.

Mrs. Dorothy Fraser, Groton, MA

The Tragedy of the *USS Indianapolis*

At 12:14 AM on July 30, 1945, the cruiser *USS Indianapolis* was torpedoed by a Japanese submarine in the Philippine Sea. It sank, bow first, in less than 15 minutes. Of the nearly 1,200 men on board, approximately 300 went down with the ship and 900 men were left floating in shark-infested waters, with few lifeboats and little food or water. By the time the survivors were rescued 5 days later, only 316 men were still alive. The rest had died from hunger, drinking salt water, drowning and shark attacks. By many accounts, this was the worst naval disaster in American history.

At the time of this attack the *USS Indianapolis* had been on her way to Leyte in the Philippines after delivering a secret cargo to Tinian Island in the Marianas. This top secret cargo reportedly was a delivery of vital parts for the atomic bombs to be dropped on Hiroshima and Nagasaki. The *Indianapolis* was due to reach Leyte on July 31, but no report was ever made when she didn't arrive on schedule, so no rescue operation was launched.

—U.S. Navy photo

By chance, a twin-engine plane flying routine patrol in the area spotted the wreckage on August 2, 1945. The pilot immediately radioed for help and rescue operations began.

The *USS Indianapolis* had traditionally served as the flagship of the 5th Fleet. Several times before the attack on Pearl Harbor, she had carried President Franklin Roosevelt and members of his cabinet. During her 14 years of service, she was honored with 10 battle stars for her actions during the war.

U.S. Drops Atomic Bomb

August 6, 1945 – A U.S. B-29, the *Enola Gay*, drops the first atomic bomb on Hiroshima.

My brother, Maurice B. Bean, guarded the *Enola Gay* for many weeks before it dropped the atomic bombs on Japan.

Mrs. Avis E. Sussenguth, Topsfield

NUCLEAR DAWN: The atomic bomb, dropped on the Japanese city of Hiroshima on Aug. 6, 1945, marked the beginning of a new era in warfare.

I will vote in honor of my father, Kendall C. Huff, who was a Seaman 1st class in WWII. He was drafted at the end of the war and was in training for the Japanese invasion when the bomb was dropped. He told me he was glad when the war was over.

Barry W. Huff, Lewiston
Served in Vietnam

Kendall C. Huff

August 9, 1945 – The second atomic bomb is dropped on **Nagasaki**.

I will be voting in honor of Maj. William Bragner, who was military governor of <u>Nagasaki</u> after the 2nd atomic bomb was dropped. Bill and I went to high school together and to Dartmouth College, where we roomed together for three years – class of 1930.

Paul F. Poehler, Wells
Served in the Navy in the Philippines

William Bragner

August 14, 1945 – The Japanese accept unconditional surrender. General MacArthur is appointed to head the occupation forces in Japan.

Mainers share personal stories about the sacrifice, valor, and dedication of servicemen and women in the Pacific Theater:

I am voting in honor of Cpl. Jack McLean, a boyhood friend of mine, who came to Maine from Vancouver, Canada, to be raised by an aunt. He subsequently ran away from her to join the Marine Corps early in WWII and was killed in the Pacific campaign.

Everett B. Perkins, Bath
Served in Army Air Corps during WWII

I am proud of the service and sacrifice of my uncle, Stanley W. Tumosa. Stan was from Dover-Foxcroft and served as a pilot in the Navy in the Pacific Fleet. On the *USS Franklin*, he was in his aircraft on deck waiting for take-off when a 500-pound bomb hit. He lost his life.

George W. Greene, Kittery Point
Served in Korea

My father, Allan E. Horne, served in the Navy during WWII on the destroyer *Vesole* that patrolled the waters near Japan. He is quite proud of the fact that he and one other aboard ship were the only ones who knew how to play cribbage. One year and a half later the whole ship knew how to play.

Janet H. Richards, Milo

Allan Horne & family
(1944)

I am voting in honor of Ben Moore, a very dear and close friend for many, many years. Ben served in the Army in the Pacific Theater, but he never talked that much about it.

Cynthia Peavey, Clinton

I want to pay tribute to both of my parents, Horace A. Howieson, now deceased, and Joan Howieson. My father was a Marine in the South Pacific and was also a gunnery/drill instructor and taught shooting. My mother was a WAVE in the U.S. Navy who worked as a lab technician stationed in San Diego.

Holly A. Howieson, Camden

I am proud of the service of my parents, Helen I. Ellis, who was a nurse in the Women's Army Corps (WAC), and Ruel P. Ellis, who was a "Sparky" in the Navy. They met each other at Fort Williams in Portland.

Ruel C. Ellis, Winthrop
Served in Vietnam and Desert Storm

I am voting in honor of my father, John E. Howe, who served in WWII, first in CAP Coastal Patrol in Portland, Maine; then he was a Navy Machinist Mate stationed in Jacksonville, Florida.

Olive E. Risko, Bryant Pond
Former cadet nurse

I am paying tribute to my father, Lyman C. Farrin, who served in the Army from 1941 to 1945 in the Pacific. My name is Victory. (Dad's Division had just won a major battle.) My dad learned of my birth in May of 1943. We have always joked that my name should have been "Furlough." I was 2 1/2 when I first met him. He is now 83 years old – a great father, husband, neighbor, grandfather, great-grandfather, veteran, and American citizen.

Victory A. Todd, Garland

Lyman C. Farrin

My father, Asa Markey, was in the Army when WWII was declared. He served many months in the Pacific Islands. One battle took place as the Japanese were eating. Dad yanked a dead Japanese soldier's face out of his dish and ate the fish and rice. He could never swallow a mouthful of tuna after WWII.

Edgar Markey, Carmel
Served in Bosnia, still serving in Army

I will be voting in honor of my father, Roscoe L. Arnold, Jr., who served on a destroyer in the South Pacific. A quiet hero!

Bruce Arnold, Greenbush
Served in Vietnam, Dominican Republic, Desert Storm
Retired E-9, US Navy

My father, John Gregory Gatchell, was only 18 years old when he served on a destroyer in the Pacific. He never talked about it, but being a veteran now myself, I know that those years had a profound effect on him.

Daniel Gary Gatchell, Brunswick
Served in Vietnam

My wife, Mabel M. Fick, served for 3 years as a 1st Lieutenant in the Army Nurse Corps in the South Pacific.

Capt. William F. Fick, Kennebunk
U.S. Army Retired

I am voting in honor of my uncle, Burton C. Treadwell, who served in the last unit of the Cavalry in WWII and was killed in Burma just before the war ended. I never knew him but because of him I'm free.

Hannah Phillips, Acton

Burton C. Treadwell

I pay tribute to my aunt, Dorothy Lombardi (Blinkhorn), who served in the WAVES.

Christina Olsen, Falmouth

My dad, Gerald Thompson, served in the Army during WWII on the Burma Road in India. I will wear the button in memory of all who have served our country, those living and those who died in my place. We owe it to our vets to take care of them and give them the peace and honor they so richly deserve.

Geraldine M. Randall, Hudson

August 16, 1945 – General Wainwright, a POW since May 6, 1942, is released from a POW camp in Manchuria.

September 2, 1945 – A formal Japanese ceremony is held on board the *USS Missouri* in Tokyo Bay as 1,000 carrier-based planes fly overhead. President Truman declares **V-J DAY**.

Flights of F4U "Corsairs" and F6F "Hellcats" over the USS Missouri (BB-63). V-J Day August 1945.

I am voting in honor of my dad, James Elmore Wright. He was a Chief Petty Officer during WWII on a battleship, the *Missouri*, I believe. He loved the Navy and was proud to serve.

Susan W. Igleheart, Old Town

My father, Kenneth A. Trafton, was serving aboard the *USS Missouri* at the signing of the peace treaty with Japan. General MacArthur was on board. My father passed away on September 1, 1999.

Mrs. Carolyn M. Gary, Mattawamkeag

I am proud of the service of my husband, James N. Bodlovick, who was a Tech 5 in the Army during WWII and was a sports writer for the Pacific *Stars and Stripes*.

Roberta P. Bodlovick, Scarborough

Wallace M. Thompson in front of tents where they slept.

My husband, Cpl. Wallace Mathew Thompson, was with the 152nd Field Artillery, 43rd Division, in the South Pacific, Coral Sea, Invasion of the Philippines, and the release of prisoners from Bataan. He served from 1943 to 1945. He got malaria and was on the seas heading for home when war was declared over…a wonderful man, devoted citizen, and honorable soldier.

Frances Schoppe Thompson, Holden

Wallace M. Thompson

My brother, Donald R. Brewster, served in the Navy from 1943 – 1945. He has always been more than just a big brother to me. He really qualifies as a hero in my book. I don't know all that he did as a Navy Pharmacist Mate, but I have heard him share just enough to know that he contributed much to the welfare of many who went onto the beaches and into the jungles in the Pacific during WWII.

Don was 18 when he went into the Navy. He had been living in Rockland with my mother and grandmother and had just graduated from Rockland High School. Our father Donald had died just a year or two before and I know that this was a tough time for Don and for my mother and grandmother. I know that his leaving was very difficult for them and that the fear of losing him after losing a husband and father was traumatic.

Donald and Virginia Brewster

I know he served aboard a hospital ship in the Pacific and that he got much of his training in Hawaii before sailing to the Pacific Theater. I know he went ashore with the Marines when they moved into the Pacific Islands. I know he was in Tokyo Harbor when the peace treaty with Japan was signed.

I know he doesn't talk much about what he saw and experienced. I believe he kept much pain to himself and I can only speculate that there were times in his life when that pain may have been difficult to bear. He is the only real father figure I have ever known and I am very proud of him and what he has done with his life.

Elbert R. Brewster, Oakland
Served in Vietnam

Battles had raged in the Pacific with heavy involvement by U.S. troops and other allied forces. The Battle of the Coral Sea in May, the Battle of Midway in June, the offensive at Guadalcanal in August, and the campaign in New Guinea in September had kept American troops fully engaged in the South Pacific.

The European Theater of Operations

"We must be ready to dare all for our country. For history does not long entrust the care of freedom to the weak or the timid. We must acquire proficiency in defense and display stamina in purpose.

We must be willing, individually and as a Nation, to accept whatever sacrifices may be required of us. A people that values its privileges above its principles soon loses both."

President Dwight D. Eisenhower (1890-1969)
First Supreme Commander of Allied Forces in World War II
34th President of the United States
First Inaugural Address, January 20, 1953

December 11, 1941 – Germany and Italy declare war on the U.S.

August 17, 1942 – The Army Air Force conducts its first raid in Europe.

Maine voters pay tribute to those in the U.S. Air Force who served in the European Theater:

I am voting in honor of Edward Ross, who was a nose gunner on a B-24 in the 8th Air Force during WWII. He received 2 Flying Crosses as well as other honors. Ed is in his 80's and still continues to work on various local committees and is active in the 8th Air Force Veterans' Association.

Donald D. Soule, York
Served in Korea

Edward Ross

I will proudly wear my "Voting in Honor of a Vet" button on my uniform when I vote this year in honor of my father, Gordon P. Gleason. He was a "farm boy" from the ancestral home in Canaan. He tried to enlist in the Army (at about age 31) but was told he was too old. A year later, he was drafted, and having worked on a tramp steamer as a radioman, he was assigned duties as a radioman on B-17 *Flying Fortress* bombers. He was sent to the Mediterranean area of Europe and North Africa in his B-17, the *Golden Hind*, replete with a huge "Vargas Girl" painted on the vertical stabilizer demurely showing off her golden panties from beneath her short, pleated skirt.

My father was a man of very few words – we never had much of a relationship while I was growing up. But as often holds true, "The older I got, the smarter he got." All he ever much said about the Army was something I overheard him say to a neighbor when I enlisted in the Army in 1968 to avoid being drafted. He told the neighbor (unaware that I was within earshot), "I fought in the last war so that my sons would never have to go to war." I was very fortunate. Though in the Army and originally trained for the infantry, I ended up serving – in the peak of the Vietnam era – in the Army's "other 'hardship' tour duty location," near the DMZ in the Republic of Korea. I've always felt that if I would have gone to Vietnam, I would never have seen Maine again.

Gordon P. Gleason

SMSgt Michael P. Gleason, Bangor
Served during Vietnam era;
currently in Maine Air Guard, USAF

Mainers warmly pay tribute to men who served in the **Merchant Marines**:

I am voting in honor of Daniel Maher and Jack Stadstad, classmates of mine at the USMMA in Kings Point, NY. Each of them was lost on their first trip to sea in 1942. Daniel Maher was on the Liberty Ship S/S *Merriwether Lewis* when it was torpedoed by a German submarine on March 2, 1943 in the North Atlantic. Jack Stadstad was on the Liberty ship S/S *John Drayton* when it was torpedoed on April 21, 1943 by an Italian submarine 300 miles southeast of Durban, South Africa.

Thomas C. Howard, Old Orchard Beach
Served in WWII

> I am proud of my grandfather, Amos Tracy, who was in the Merchant Marines during WWII. He fought this war for our freedom. His country was his pride.
>
> *Sylvia Merry, Old Orchard Beach*

> I am voting in honor of my grandfather, David V. McCallum, who was in the Merchant Marines. After the war, at age 42, he fell from a telephone pole and became a quadriplegic. He was told he would never have the use of his arms and legs. Through sheer will and constant trying, he regained the use of his arms, but he was never able to walk again.
>
> He had no income and a wife and 3 children to support. But, with the help of some people from Old Orchard Beach he sold sea worms from his house. Later he opened the OOB Tent and Trailer Park and let people camp for donations only.
>
> He hunted, fished, and lived a full life. He even deep sea fished. He would go to the Camp Ellis pier and they would attach straps to his wheel chair and they would hoist him up, out and over the water on to his boat. He was fearless.
>
> He was never limited by his body because of his incredible mind and spirit. He passed away in 1990. His spirit will live forever.
>
> *Roxanne V. McCallum-Frenette, Old Orchard Beach*

Americans Face Action on the Southern Front: North Africa, Morocco, Tunisia, Algeria

November 7, 1942 – U.S. forces land in North Africa, and **Operation Torch**, the North African campaign, begins.

*Sons and daughters pay tribute to **fathers**:*

> Our father, Paul A. Rovnak, served in the U.S. Army Air Corps in WWII. He lost an eye during the war in Northern Africa but never once complained.
>
> *Mary-Ann Rovnak Morgan, Lisbon Falls*

I am voting in honor of my father, Charles W. Kauffman, who was a veteran of WWII; he served as an Army sergeant with the 102nd Infantry Division.

Sandy Bates, Greene

Charles W. Kauffman

I will vote in honor of my father, James Robert Blanch, who went into the CC's at 17 years old and later shipped out to serve in WWII on Christmas Eve. He was in the Army and is still very active in the local VFW. He takes a great deal of pride in the military part of his life but unfortunately does not share many stories.

Laura Cook, West Enfield

*Husbands, WWII veterans themselves, vote in honor of their **wives**:*

Emelda B. Erwin, my wife, was an Army nurse during WWII and served in Africa and Italy.

Edgar E. Erwin, Rumford
Served in England, Africa and Italy during WWII

Emelda B. Erwin

My wife, Marilynn B. Gage, was an Ensign in the Navy Nurse Corps during my stay in the U.S. Naval Hospital in Boston. (We have now been married for 54 years.)

Wallace M. Gage, Tenants Harbor
Served in Battle of the Atlantic,
Aleutians, and Saipan, USN (Ret.)

I vote in honor of my wife, Kathleen M. Moore, who became a naturalized citizen of the United States but served in the British Army as a radio operator monitoring enemy radio signals. One of the girls in her unit intercepted the change in the German code. (I believe this is indirectly mentioned in *The Ultra Secret* by F. W. Winterbotham.)

Donald E. Moore, Ellsworth
Served in the Pacific Theater during WWII

My wife, Genevieve Leone Sirois (now deceased), was a WAC in WWII.

Sebastian Fred Sirois, No. Monmouth
Served in WWII and Korean Conflict

I am voting in honor of my wife, Pauline G. Paul, who was a Storekeeper Second Class in the U.S. Navy WAVES.

Peter F. Paul, Saco
Served in WWII

My wife, Janet S. Vincent (now deceased) was a WAVE PHM 3/c USN who served in the U.S. and Hawaii.

Vernon R. Vincent, North Waterford
Served in WWII and Korea

Janet S. Vincent

I pay tribute to my wife, Cpl. Olive F. Parent (now deceased), who was in the U.S. Marines in 1941-42.

Albert E. Parent, Oakland
Served in the U.S. Army, 1955-58

I am proud to vote in honor of my wife, Margaret L. Ford, who was a WAVE in the U.S. Navy during WWII and served in communications at USNAS in Jacksonville, Florida.

John F. Ford, Sr., Alfred
Served in North Africa, France,
the Rhineland, and Ardennes

Margaret L Ford

*Wives proudly pay tribute to their **husbands**:*

I am voting in honor of my husband, Milton S. Jellison, who served with the 1st Infantry Division in the U.S. Army and participated in battles and campaigns in Algeria, Morocco and Tunisia. He was captured by the Germans at the Battle of Kasserine Pass in North Africa, where it is a widely held belief that his actions on that day saved many soldiers from a similar fate, or worse. He was taken prisoner and held at Oflag 64 in Poland from 1943 to 1945. In recognition of his service and bravery, he was awarded the Silver Star, African-Middle Eastern Theater Service medals, and the Bronze Service Arrowhead.

Dorothy P. Jellison, Bangor

Lawrence A. Michaud

I will vote in honor of my husband, Lawrence A. Michaud, who is a WWII veteran. He served in both the African and European Theaters and received 4 battle stars. He spoke at an elementary school on Veterans' Day regarding the importance of our flag and our freedoms. Students wrote letters stating they had learned more about our constitution and our flag from his speeches than they did in the classroom.

Maurine S. Michaud, Ashland

*Many responses to **Vote in Honor of a Veteran** reveal admiration for relationships that lasted lifetimes:*

Victor Smallidge was my good friend and fellow lobster fisherman. He served in the U.S. Army in WWII. He landed in Africa and fought in Italy…claiming he walked the whole way …a true "foot soldier."

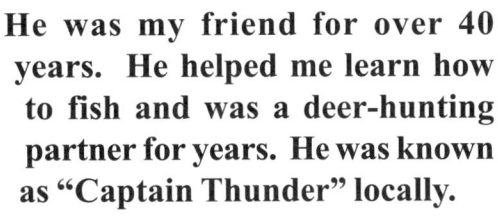

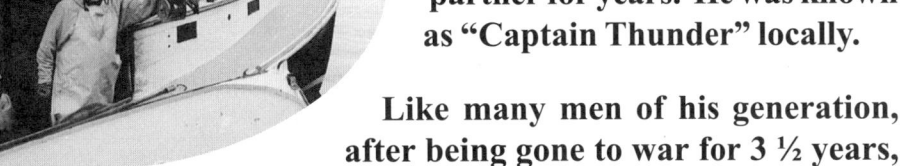

He was my friend for over 40 years. He helped me learn how to fish and was a deer-hunting partner for years. He was known as "Captain Thunder" locally.

Like many men of his generation, after being gone to war for 3 ½ years, he returned home to Winter Harbor and resumed his life of fishing. He spoke little of the battles, but was vocal in relating how the GIs would give their food to the children they met.

Victor Smallidge

Dale F. Torrey, Sr., Winter Harbor
Served in the Army

My cousin, Henry Howe, was a sergeant in WWII in the U.S. Army Air Corps in the European Theater. He helped save the Lipizzaner stallions.

Sandy Bates, Greene

Henry Howe

I am voting in honor of Pastor Stanley Royal Ashby, Jr., my brother-in-law. He was a graduate of Harvard and could speak 6 to 7 languages fluently. He taught Chinese and Korean in the military. He was a humble but brilliant man of God.

John Franklin Bixby Jr., Buckfield
Served in Vietnam

73

July 19, 1943 – The Allies bomb Rome, which had previously been spared because of its religious significance.

August 17, 1943 – General Patton and his troops conquer Sicily.

September 1943 – The Allies invade Italy. Italy surrenders, but German forces in the country continue to fight. The U.S. Army lands at Salerno, Italy.

I am voting in honor of my brother, Robert L. Leavitt, who was drafted at the end of the war and served in the Infantry in Italy. He died in 1944 and left behind a young wife and baby boy. When he died, I was only 9 years old. We all miss him still.

Dorothy L. Benner, Gardiner

Robert L. Leavitt

I will proudly pay tribute to my father, William R. Foley, who served in WWII and was stationed in Italy. He worked in a MASH unit. He was a Canadian citizen and became naturalized before shipping out.

Marybeth Foley, Orient

When I vote, I will be paying tribute to my father, Horace (Bud) White, who served in WWII in the 5th Army. He went through Italy and Africa and was at the foot of the Alps when the war ended.

Even bad times have their funny moments. In Italy he became acquainted with a man from Maine – and they are still good friends despite the distance between their homes. One evening after dark, Dad and Bill were returning to their platoon when the Germans launched an air attack on the area. Not being armed to fight off planes, all they could do was dive for cover under the nearest available source, which happened to be a military truck. They had "procured" some wine to share with their buddies, and, not knowing if they'd ever see daylight again, they opened a bottle and drank some while the attack was on.

Horace (Bud) White

When the attack finally ended, they crawled out from under the truck, only to find it was fully loaded with ammunition. One stray bullet would have been the last for them, but Divine intervention saved them that day.

Deedra R. Davis, Bangor

January 22, 1944 – The Allies land at Anzio, Italy.

*Mainers honor those who fought at **Anzio**:*

> Charles Dube, who was born in Caribou, Maine, saved my life. It was February, 1944. The Germans had surrounded the house I was in. When Charles fired his gun, 2 ran from the house.
>
> *Gerard E. Chretien, Alfred*
> *Served in WWII, fought at Anzio*

> I am voting in honor of my husband, Joseph Glenn Grover, who enlisted in the Navy in 1942 and served as a torpedo man on several destroyers, including the *USS Bristol* and the *USS Ludlow*. He was involved with the Anzio invasion in 1944 and also with the invasion of Salerno. He was the father of 6 and died in 1973 just before his 52nd birthday.
>
> *Muriel Grover, Passadumkeag*

Joseph G. Grover

*Proud wives vote in tribute to their **husbands'** valor:*

> My husband, Staff Sergeant Meryll M. Frost, was a ball turret gunner on a B-24 bomber, 15th Air Force, 726 Bomber Squadron, 451st Bomber Group. His B-24 crashed on a mission overseas in February 1944. It caught fire and 2 ½ tons of bombs exploded. Most of the crew was killed instantly, leaving only a few alive. My husband was severely burned and injured and hospitalized for 1½ years in military hospitals. He was listed as 100% disabled and was given a Purple Heart.
>
> *Mrs. Pauline D. Frost, Columbia Falls*

> For the past 55 years my husband, George E. Tudor, has kept in touch with his crew; eight are still living. Most will be attending the 451st bomb group reunion in September in St. Louis. The missions they went through – and survived – are unbelievable. He has been an A-1 husband and father as he was a pilot. After he was discharged from the Air Force, he flew for 32 years with American Airlines.
>
> *Jane Tudor, Bristol*

Note: According to General Order #4533, dated 17 November 1944, for "conspicuous gallantry, professional skill and intense devotion to duty," Captain George Tudor was awarded the Silver Star for gallantry.

George E. Tudor

I am married to a wonderful man, Elvert G. Pooler, who wears the Purple Heart with enormous pride. He served in the U.S. Army from 1943 to 1945, served in France and Germany, and was wounded twice. He received the Bronze Star and the Purple Heart with 2 Oak Leaf Clusters.

Barbara B. Pooler, Sanford

Elvert G. Pooler

*Sons and daughters honor their **mothers** and **grandmothers**:*

I want to honor my mom, Naomi M. Watts, who was a wing tip riveter – a "Rosie the Riveter" – during WWII. She helped win the war by providing needed services on the home front.

Laura M. Duplessis, Old Town

Naomi M. Watts

I am proud of my mother, Jeannette Campbell, who was a clerk in the Women's Army Corps and a gate guard at Andrews Field during WWII. After the war she served as the postmaster in Bingham until her retirement in 1987.

Kevin Campbell, Dresden
Served in USMC, 1972-78

Jeannette Campbell

When I vote, I will do so in honor of my grandmother, Andrea Melness, who served in the U.S. Navy Nurse Corps during WWII.

Thomas F. Malone III, Portland
Served in the Gulf War

I am voting in honor of my mother, Captain Helen Williams, who served in England in the U.S. Army Nurse Corps for 3 years. She was one of 4 siblings who served in WWII.

Kendall N. Huggins, Bangor

I honor my grandmother, Susie Buck, who served as a WAC in WWII.

Wilma F. Buck Warman, Belmont

An article provided by Beatrice Kelleter reports on the fate of her cousin, a lost pilot:

"First Lieutenant Philip S. Wood, Jr., (Air Forces, United States Army) went overseas in January of 1944 and was stationed with the 15th Air Force in Southern Italy. He was the pilot of a B24 Liberator Bomber that failed to return after a bombing mission over Vienna. He was awarded the Distinguished Flying Cross.

Lt. Wood was reported missing in action on the 17th of March 1944. The War Department had entertained the hope that he had survived and that information would be revealed dispelling the uncertainty surrounding his absence. No further information has been received."

Beatrice Kelleter, West Gouldsboro
A cousin of Lt. Wood

—the *Bar Harbor Times*, August 9, 1945

The following Associated Press report of May 7, 2001 from Presque Isle, Maine, brings memories of the war to a downed pilot:

FORMER MAINER GIVEN PLANE PARTS AS REMINDER OF WW II CRASH

Fifty years ago, George Peterson was shot down near Linz, Austria, during World War II, and became a prisoner of war.

Now the former Maine resident has received a bittersweet artifact from that experience: two metal pieces of the plane he was in when he was shot down.

Peterson, 85, received the parts of the B-24 Liberator from two Austrian men who are compiling a history of the day his and about a dozen other planes were shot down on July 25, 1944.

"It brings back past memories and what we went through," Peterson said. "No one can understand unless they've gone through it."

Peterson grew up in northern Maine and was living in New Sweden when he was drafted. He was 27 years old when he was sent to Italy, where he worked as a flight engineer on the plane. There were 10 members of the Liberator crew who flew together for two years during the war, and until July 25, the plane had only received a few bullet holes during the war.

But on the crew's 44th mission, they were one of 21 planes attacked as they approached Linz. The crew bailed out of the plane by parachute, and became prisoners of war.

He spent the next nine months in several concentration camps in Austria, Poland and Germany before being rescued by British soldiers.

Hundreds of acts of heroism during WWII are described in the responses honoring veterans. Here is a sampling:

> My grandfather, Ken Joy, received the Bronze Star for crawling around and behind a bunch of German soldiers. He threw a hand grenade and wiped them out and saved his pinned-down comrades.
>
> *Joy Lynne Colby, Springvale*

> I will be voting in honor of my shipmate, David Niles Skinner, who served in WWII on the *USS Rolfe* as a Gunner's Mate 3rd class. He was lost at sea in the Atlantic in November 1944. He was a most respected sailor, missed by his shipmates. He never had the opportunity to gain his "veteran" status.
>
> *Donald W. Pratt, Freeport*
> *Served in U.S. Navy during WWII*

> I want to pay tribute to my uncle, Jack R. Craig, who was inducted into the Army shortly after his graduation from high school in 1943. He served in combat in WWII, was wounded 3 times and received the Purple Heart. He recently celebrated his 50th wedding anniversary. He is an unrecognized hero!
>
> *Ted L. Igleheart, Old Town*
> *Served in Persian Gulf, Somalia, and Haiti*

> I am voting in honor of my parents. My father, Myron Prescott (now deceased), was a bombardier on B-52s and earned the Flying Cross and Purple Heart with Silver Star. My mother, Jane Prescott, was born and raised in France and worked with the French underground saving Jews.
>
> *James M. Prescott, South Portland*
> *Combat-wounded in Vietnam*

> My father, William See, served in the 8th Air Force, 95th Bomb Group, 336th Squadron, as a Flight Engineer on a B-17. He was shot down on his 11th mission. My father walked on a forced march over 600 kilometers across Germany. He has never received his POW medal. He will be 80 years <u>young</u> on December 14, 2000. I am so proud of my father and what he did, not only for me but also for what he did for our great country.

William See

> *Daniel See, Bucksport*

I am voting in honor of my uncle, George Ernest Boisse, who served one tour in the Navy and then joined the Air Force, planning to make his career in the Air Force. He was a radio operator during WWII.

George E. Boisse

The details of his story may not be exact because we never heard the story firsthand. I've heard this story since I was a child but never from my Uncle George. He never spoke about it. He had never even spoken about it with his wife of over fifty years. He told his mother what happened when she was by his side in the hospital recuperating from his ordeal. My grandmother is the person who shared this story of courage and character with his wife and close family members.

One day during a flight his airplane was shot down. One man died on impact and another lost half of his leg, but my uncle was not injured. My uncle pulled the injured man into a life raft. The two men were adrift in the ocean with no food and very little water. My uncle wrapped the injured man's leg with a shirt he had. The gentleman died three days later. Because of aroused sharks in the area, my uncle had no choice but to place the gentleman's body into the water.

On the sixteenth day he saw an airplane fly overhead, but the airplane didn't tip its wing to alert my Uncle George that the airplane had seen him. At that point he prayed for the Good Lord to take him because he thought he would not be rescued. He was severely dehydrated, sunburned, and suffering from heat stroke. The very next day a ship came to rescue him. He was hospitalized for the next few months recuperating. In all, he had spent 17 days adrift in the ocean.

My uncle was heartbroken about having to leave the gentleman's body in the ocean. He and his wife were expecting their first child. When my uncle received his Purple Heart, he gave it to the wife of the gentleman who died so his child would have it to remember his brave father.

I am glad my grandmother shared this story about this touching life experience of a dedicated member of the U.S. Air Force. We are very proud to call such an honorable man our uncle.

Brenda J. Paquette, Biddeford

I met my husband Gustave Delannoy, Jr. while we both served at Anacostia Naval Air Station in Washington, D.C. I served stateside while Gus fought the war. He spent 14 days in a life raft in the North Atlantic in winter months during the first bombing.

Julia Delannoy, North Amity
Served stateside in the Navy in WWII

My dad, Gustave Delannoy Jr., was a "tin can" sailor. He made all the invasions of WWII. He was sunk twice and was decorated for his heroic rescue of a shipmate. Dad died 2 days before his 75th birthday in 1996 and is buried at Arlington Cemetery.

George C. Delannoy, North Amity
Served in Vietnam

On December 24, 1944, the troopship *SS Leopoldville*, carrying some 2,000 U.S. servicemen, was torpedoed just five and a half miles from its destination in Cherbourg, France. 763 soldiers, all members of the 66th Infantry Division, were killed. In addition, 650 of the 1,400 survivors were injured. Among the casualties was my father, Edward F. Stone of Brownville, Maine. He was only 23 years old at the time. He left behind his wife, three sons, and two daughters. I was only 6 months old when he was killed.

The soldiers that lost their lives deserve the proper remembrance for their sacrifice and those that survived need to be recognized for their valor. We must protect their final resting place from desecration and instead exhibit American artifacts from the *Leopoldville* as a memorial to the Americans who gave their lives in the fight against tyranny.

Virginia G. Weston, Brownville Junction

When I vote, I will honor my friend Jack Gault, who served in the U.S. Army in WWII and died in Germany. Jack was one of the 97 male graduates (out of 99) in the high school class of 1942 who served in the armed services in WWII.

Keith E. Miller, Bar Harbor
Served in WWII

Jack Gault

Lowell F. Simmons

I am voting in honor of my brother, Second Lt. Lowell F. Simmons, who was an Air Force pilot of a B-17 that dropped bombs on Berlin. His plane was hit by flak that knocked out 3 engines. My brother ordered the other 9 men to jump. They were captured but the war was at an end so they returned home. My brother, however, did not. His chute caught on the tail wing of the plane and he went down with it. For his valor in battle he was awarded the Purple Heart. He was 27 years old and the father of 2 children. Today his body is buried in the family plot in Damariscotta with other loved ones.

Gloria S. Knipe, New Harbor

Vernon A. Fuller

My father, Vernon A. Fuller, served in the Army in Germany during WWII and was shot and wounded during action. True and loyal to his country, he never tried to receive a disability for his injuries although he easily could have. He believed in loyalty and loyalty alone and dedication to his country.

Vivian M. Fuller, Belfast
Serving in Maine Army
National Guard, with duty in
Vietnam, Desert Storm, and Bosnia

Vernon A. Fuller

My grandfather, Kenneth E. Joy, served two terms in Germany during WWII. He was the proud recipient of a Purple Heart as well as many other medals. He was a great man. He is sadly missed.

Carole-Ann Labbe, Shapleigh

My cousin, Walter Meader, was a B-24 gunner, killed in action over Germany. He was the first soldier KIA from the Passamaquoddy Reservation.

Richard J. Socabasin, Sr., Perry
Served in WWII, Korea, and Vietnam,
US Army (Ret.)

Thank you for the opportunity to honor my father Ralph E. Berry. He died November 17, 1978. I pulled out the box of his military service memorabilia for the 100th time and looked at the two awards (the Bronze Star Medal and the Purple Heart Medal) he received April 30, 1945 "for heroic conduct in connection with military operations against an army enemy" on March 31, 1945.

CITATION

"Technician Fourth Grade Ralph E. Berry, 41st Tank Battalion, 11th Armored Division, United States Army. For heroic conduct in connection with military operation against an armed enemy. On 31 March 1945, while serving as tank gunner for his unit near Fulda, Germany, Technician Berry's tank was hit by an enemy bazooka round. He was severely burned about the hands and his company commander was mortally wounded. Hoping to get his Company Commander back to the aid station, Technician Berry, discovering that his driver had lost his interphone headset, leaned out of the turret to instruct him, thus exposing himself to heavy enemy sniper fire. His conduct was in keeping with the highest traditions of the United States Army. Technician Berry entered the military service from Maine."

Iva M. Berry, Rangeley

Gerard E. Turgeon

I am voting in honor of my father, Gerard E. Turgeon, who served in the U.S. Army 3rd Armored Division Spearhead Infantry in Belgium and France. He was wounded in both of his legs and his back on December 14, 1944 in Germany and nearly lost a leg. He received a Purple Heart. He says he would do it again.

Michael G. Turgeon, Shapleigh
Served in Desert Storm, a 10-year veteran

When I vote, I will pay tribute to my father, Llewellyn Fowler Wortman, who served in the U.S. Army in France from 1943 – 1945. He was drafted even though he had 6 children. There were no support services for dependents during WWII, which made life difficult for those left behind.

Patricia A. Sherman, Olamon

Acts of heroism sometimes resulted in capture and imprisonment:

> **I am voting in honor of all veterans. I was a Bombardier-Navigator, shot down and parachuted in 1943. I remained in (prison camp) Stalag Luft until May 1945.**
>
> *Albert L. Farrah, Kittery Point*
> Served in WWII

> **My friend, Forest Crosman (now deceased), was a U.S. Air Force B-17 radioman, who was shot down over Germany. He was a POW for many months and lost 100 pounds in POW camp.**
>
> *Frank E. DeBiasio, Jr., Topsham*
> Served in the Pacific with the 3rd Fleet, 1944-45

> **My brother, Lionel Crocker, served in the Army and was held prisoner of war in Germany. A man 6' tall, he weighed about 90 pounds when he came home.**
>
> *James F. Crocker, Exeter*

> **I am voting in honor of my "survival brother" Alvin L. Tidwell. We were both POW's together in Germany – AUS Infantry.**
>
> *Murray A. Schwartz, Mechanic Falls*
> Served in WWII

> **I am proud of my husband, Warren G. McFadden, who served in the Air Force. He was a POW from 1943-45 in Stalag Luft 17B in Germany. He died August 17th, 1996 on our 50th anniversary. I am happy to honor him...he was a good man.**
>
> *Arlene R. McFadden, Harpswell*

Many responses from Maine voters celebrated the contributions of WWII veterans on the Western Front in Germany, France, Austria, Luxembourg, and Belgium:

> **I pay tribute to the service of my father, Wayne St. Germain, who served in Germany. He parachuted behind enemy lines and was hidden in a farmhouse by a German family. He did see combat and was wounded.**
>
> *Lorelei St. Germain, Mt. Desert*

> **All in my family who served are gone now except me. I served in the U.S. Army in Germany and southern France from September 1944 to October 1946. When I vote, I will wear my button to honor "all who served with me."**
>
> *Dominic J. D'Andrea, Lisbon*
> Served in WWII

I am voting in honor of S/Sgt. Charles T. Bratton. He was the tail gunner of our bomber crew and was killed in aerial combat with the enemy in late 1944. May God reward him for all the good things he has done.

Romeo A. Huppe, Lewiston
Served in aerial combat missions during WWII

My grandfather, Bernal Clark, served with the 258th Engineer Battalion in the U.S. Army during WWII. He was someone who was very wise and honorable. I loved him very much and learned a lot of things from him.

Denise M. Hitchcock, Smyrna Mills

Bernal Clark

My brother, William Willard (Woody) McKinney, Jr., was a paramedic and paratrooper. He joined the Army against his mother's wishes saying, "I must do my part for my country."

Lou Ann Cranouski, Thorndike

Thomas Andrews served in the Army in Germany. I have talked with him personally about searching for landmines with his bayonet. He is a silent type who did his duty to the utmost.

Dennis E. Perry, Sorrento

Sorties were operational flights by a single military aircraft.

I will be voting for the first time at college and will be proud to vote in honor of my grandfather, Albert Grivois, who was in the USAF in WWII and flew in over 80 sorties.

Julie York, Durham, NH

I will be proud to wear the name of SMSgt. Harry Stiefel, USAF, when I vote on Election Day. I met him in 1961 at Supreme Headquarters Allied Powers, Europe, in Paris, France, where we were stationed with a small Strategic Air Command (SAC) unit. Over the next four years our two New England families became very friendly – we planned and went on trips together, we had baked bean and spaghetti suppers together on Saturday nights, we played cards together, we bowled together.

Harry was a true gentleman, a kind man thoughtful and caring; he was very devoted to his wife and children, to his religion, and to his country.

His devotion to duty and country was recognized officially by both the United States government and the government of France. During WWII Harry was a waist gunner on a B-26 Marauder and flew 26 missions over Germany. On one mission the bombardier radioed the pilot that one of the bombs had failed to deploy and was hung up in the well. Harry volunteered to go into the well, bomb doors wide open, and disengaged the stuck bomb with his outstretched foot. His tireless and courageous efforts to unseat the bomb were successful and the airplane and crew were able to land safely. In addition to his U.S. medals, Harry received the French Croix de Guerre (awarded for bravery in action.)

Harry Stiefel

Kenneth B. McGrath, Eddington

I will be voting in honor of my four brothers, Thomas, Alymer, Harry and John Evans. All of them served in different units in the European Theater, and two of them were wounded.

Edith M. Wietzke, Hartland

I pay tribute to my uncle, Frank Rush. He served in Europe in the Army during WWII. He is a man that I respect, a man who is a Christian, a man who went in harm's way. He is a loved one that I have not seen in many years.

William A. Rush, Stetson
Served in Vietnam

"The Medal of Honor is the highest award for valor in action against an enemy force which can be bestowed upon an individual serving in the Armed Services of the United States. Generally presented to its recipient by the President of the United States of America in the name of Congress, it is often called the Congressional Medal of Honor."

Since its inception in 1861, the Congressional Medal of Honor has been awarded to 3,436 recipients.

As of April 2001, 149 recipients of the Congressional Medal of Honor are still living: 61 from World War II, 21 from the Korean Conflict, and 67 from the Vietnam Conflict.

This information is provided by the Congressional Medal of Honor Society. For additional information on the medal, its symbolism, its history and an entire list of recipients, you may visit the Society's website at http://www.cmohs.org.

A list of all **Maine** Medal of Honor recipients is included at the end of this book.

When I vote, I will be paying tribute to Edward C. Dahlgren, 2nd Lt., Company E, 142nd Infantry, 36th Infantry Division. He currently lives in Mars Hill.

Robert M. Henderson, Caribou
Served in Sicily, Italy, and France

I will be voting in honor of Edward C. Dahlgren, Medal of Honor recipient.

Joseph C. Rump, Bucksport
Served in Korea and Vietnam,
M. Sgt. USAF, (Ret.)

Edward C. Dahlgren

The Citation presented to Sergeant Edward C. Dahlgren on September 10, 1945, for his acts of heroism at Oberhoffen, France on February 11, 1945 reads as follows:

CITATION

"He led the Third Platoon to the rescue of a similar unit which had been surrounded in an enemy attack at Oberhoffen, France. As he advanced along a street, he observed several Germans crossing a field about 100 yards away. Running into a barn, he took up a position in a window and swept the hostile troops with submachine gun fire, killing six, wounding others and completely disorganizing the group. His platoon then moved forward through intermittent sniper fire and made contact with the besieged Americans. When the two platoons had been reorganized, Sergeant Dahlgren continued to advance along the street until he drew fire from an enemy-held house. In the face of machine-pistol and rifle fire, he ran toward the building, hurled a grenade through the door, and blasted his way inside with his gun. This attack so rattled the Germans that all eight men who held the strongpoint immediately surrendered. As Sergeant Dahlgren started toward the next house, hostile machine-gun fire drove him to cover. He secured rifle grenades, stepped to an exposed position, and calmly launched his missiles from a difficult angle until he had destroyed the machine gun and killed its two operators. He moved to the rear of the house and suddenly came under the fire of a machine gun emplaced in a barn. Throwing a grenade into the structure, he rushed the position, firing his weapon as he ran; within, he overwhelmed five Germans. After reorganizing his unit, he advanced to clear hostile riflemen from the building where he had destroyed the machine gun. He entered the house by a window and trapped the Germans in the cellar, where he tossed grenades into their midst, wounding several and forcing ten more to surrender. While reconnoitering another street with a comrade, he heard German voices in a house. An attack with rifle grenades drove the hostile troops to the cellar. Sergeant Dahlgren entered the building, kicked open the cellar door, and firing several bursts down the stairway, called for the trapped enemy to surrender. Sixteen soldiers filed out with their hands in the air. The bold leadership and magnificent courage displayed by Sergeant Dahlgren in his heroic attacks were in a large measure responsible for repulsing an enemy counterattack and saving an American platoon from great danger."

Maine Medal of Honor Recipients from World War II

In addition to Edward C. Dahlgren, four other Maine veterans received the distinguished Medal of Honor and one serviceman, who entered service in Massachusetts, is a current Maine resident.

Sergeant William C. Fournier, of Winterport, served in the U.S. Army, Company M, 35th Infantry, 25th Infantry Division at Guadalcanal, Solomon Islands on June 5, 1943, as a "leader of a machinegun section charged with the protection of other battalion units. His group was attacked by a superior number of Japanese, his gunner killed, his assistant gunner wounded, an adjoining gun crew put out of action...Sergeant Fournier rushed forward to the idle gun and, with the aid of another soldier who joined him, held up the machinegun by the tripod to increase his field of action. They opened fire and inflicted heavy casualties upon the enemy. While so engaged both these gallant soldiers were killed, but their sturdy defensive action was a decisive factor in the following success of the attacking battalion."

Commander Herbert E. Schonland, of Portland, served in the U.S. Navy on the *USS San Francisco*. He received the Medal of Honor "for extreme heroism and courage above and beyond the call of duty as damage control officer in action against greatly superior enemy forces in the battle of Savo Island, 12 November 1942...In a violent night engagement all of his superior officers were killed or wounded...Upon being informed that he was commanding officer, ... he resumed the vitally important work maintaining the stability of the ship. In water waist deep, he carried on his efforts in darkness illuminated only by hand lanterns until water in flooded compartments had been drained or pumped off and watertight integrity had again been restored...His great personal valor and gallant devotion to duty at great peril to his own life were instrumental in bringing his ship back to port under her own power, saved to fight again in the service of her country."

First Lieutenant Robert T. Waugh, who entered the service in Augusta, served in the U.S. Army, 339th Infantry, 85th Infantry Division. He received the Medal of Honor "for conspicuous gallantry and intrepidity at risk of life above and beyond the call of duty in action with the enemy." Near Tremensucli, Italy, on May 11, 1944, 1st Lt. Waugh directed his men "to deliver fire on six bunkers" guarding a hill in a heavily mined area. 1st Lt. Waugh advanced alone against them, reached the first bunker, threw three phosphorus grenades into it and as the defenders emerged, killed them with a burst from his tommy gun. He repeated this process on the five remaining bunkers, killing or capturing the occupants...The fearless actions of 1st Lt. Waugh broke the Gustav Line at that point, neutralizing six bunkers and two pillboxes and he was personally responsible for the deaths of 30 of the enemy and the capture of 25 others. He was later killed in action in Itri, Italy, while leading his platoon in an attack."

Major Jay Zeamer, Jr., who entered the military in Machias, served in the U.S. Army Air Corps. He received the Medal of Honor for service in the Solomon Islands on June 16, 1943. Major Zeamer (then Captain) volunteered as a pilot of a bomber on an important photographic mapping mission covering the formidably defended area in the vicinity of Buka, Solomon Islands. While photographing the Buka airdrome, his crew observed about 20 enemy fighters on the field, many of them taking off...Major Zeamer proceeded with the mapping run, even after the enemy attack began. In the ensuing engagement Major Zeamer sustained gunshot wounds in both arms and legs, one leg being broken. Despite his injuries, he maneuvered the damaged plane so skillfully that his gunners were able to fight off the enemy during a running fight which lasted 40 minutes. The crew destroyed at least five hostile planes, of which Major Zeamer shot down one. Although weak from loss of blood, he refused medical aid until the enemy had broken combat. He then turned over the controls, but continued to exercise command despite lapses into unconsciousness and directed the flight to a base 580 miles away. In this voluntary action, Major Zeamer, with superb skill, resolution, and courage, accomplished a mission of great value."

*Major Zeamer, one of the four surviving Maine Medal of Honor recipients, currently resides in Boothbay Harbor.

Captain Everett Parker Pope entered the service in Massachusetts but was born in Belgrade, Maine, and, as such, is listed as a recipient of a Special Citation from Maine as a Medal of Honor recipient for his service in the U.S. Marine Corps, Company C, 1st Battalion, 1st Marines, 1st Marine Division. On Peleliu Island September 18-20, 1944, "his valiant leadership against devastating odds while protecting the units below from heavy Japanese attack reflects the highest credit upon Captain Pope and the U.S. Naval Service."

*Captain Pope currently lives in Belgrade Lakes.

Everett Pope, Lewis Millett, Jay Zeamer, Edward Dahlgren

Prelude to "Operation Overload"

"During the first six months of 1944, the United States and Great Britain concentrated land, naval, and air forces in England to prepare for Operation Overload. While the Soviet Union tied down a great portion of the enemy's forces, the western Allies marshalled their resources, trained their forces separately and jointly for the operation, and designed the invasion plans to take full advantage of their joint and combined capabilities.

"Before the invasion, the air and sea components played major roles. The 12,000 planes of the Allied air forces swept the Luftwaffe from the skies, photographed enemy defenses, dropped supplies to the resistance, bombed railways, attacked Germany's industries and isolated the battlefield. The Allies' naval component was similarly active during the buildup. The navies escorted convoys, patrolled and protected the English Channel, reconnoitered beaches and beach defenses, conducted amphibious rehearsals and organized and loaded a mighty flotilla to land the assault forces in France.

"Meanwhile, the nine army divisions (three airborne and six infantry) from the United States, Britain, and Canada trained and rehearsed their roles in the carefully choreographed operation. Rangers climbed cliffs, engineers destroyed beach obstacles, quartermasters stockpiled supplies and infantrymen waded through the English surf as each honed the skills necessary for the invasion's success."

— "Fact Sheet D-Day, 6 June 1944 Normandy, France" at www.ukans.edu/heritage

"D-Day" is a military term designating the start date for launching an operation, but in modern history it is assumed to refer to the events of June 6, 1944. **Overload** is the official name for this particular operation.

June 6, 1944: Allies Invade the Beaches at Normandy

"The build-up in the British Isles was easily the most tremendous single logistical undertaking of all time. Preparations included transporting some 1,600,000 men across the submarine-infested Atlantic and providing their shelter, hospitalization, supply, training, and general welfare.

"Despite a weather forecast of high winds and a rough sea, General Eisenhower made a fateful decision to go ahead with the invasion on June 6. During the night over 5,000 ships moved to assigned positions, and at two o'clock, the operation for which the world had long and anxiously waited began…The first waves of infantry and tanks began to touch down at 6:30, just after sunrise."

— *Chapter 22,* **World War II: The War Against Germany and Italy** *by Charles B. MacDonald*

—*U.S. Army photo*

More than 5,000 Allied ships steamed through 10 lanes cleared by minesweepers. The warships opened fire with the most intense bombardment in naval history.

In the invasion's early hours, more than 1,000 transports dropped paratroopers to secure the flanks and beach exits of the assault area.

I pay tribute to Pfc. Richard George Tanner, who parachuted into France on D-Day, June 6, 1944, and was killed in action 28 days later.

Lloyd F. Coombs, Woolwich

I cast my vote in tribute to my father, Freeman Gushee, who is 79 years *young* and very active. My parents live in Belfast where he still works part-time doing carpentry work, and in October he and my mother will celebrate their 58th wedding anniversary. I just read for the first time the following newspaper article, dated August 16, 1945, about his military service during WWII:

"T/Sgt. Freeman Gushee, son of Mr. And Mrs. Robert Gushee of Appleton and husband of Daisy Roberts Gushee of Swanville, has been awarded the Bronze Star Medal for distinguishing himself by meritorious service in connection with military operations against an enemy of the United States from July 4, 1944 to May 8, 1945, in France, Luxembourg, Belgium and Germany.

Sergeant Gushee fulfilled his duty as a rifle platoon Sergeant in an excellent manner, displaying high traits of initiative and aggressiveness on more than one occasion. He took command of a platoon when the leader became a casualty. He led many patrols and successfully led his men in many attacks, reaching his assigned objectives. He was wounded during one engagement. Sgt. Gushee refused to be evacuated but remained at his post. The courage, unswerving devotion to duty and aggressiveness shown by Sgt. Gushee reflect great credit to himself and the armed forces of the United States."

Freeman Gushee

Rhonda Stark, Canaan

During **Operation Overload**, the Allies landed at five beaches, with the code names of Utah, Omaha, Gold, Juno, and Sword, in the Normandy area on the northwest coast of France. In the eastern zone, the British and Canadians landed on Gold, Juno, and Sword Beaches. The Americans landed on two beaches in the west – Utah and Omaha.

U.S. soldiers began wading 100 yards to **Utah Beach**. Ten miles to the east at **Omaha Beach**, heavy German defenses on the bluffs above killed 4,649 U.S. troops who were trying to secure the beachhead. British and Canadian troops pushed ashore against lighter defenses and over easier terrain on Gold, Juno, and Sword beaches.

Maine veterans land on beaches far from home:

I will be voting in honor of my brother, Carlton E. Hutchins, who was in the U.S. Infantry at the Battle of Normandy, landing on <u>Utah Beach.</u> He was with his Division all of his time, going to the Margenot Line and on to Pelsen, Czechoslovakia. He was hospitalized for frozen feet. He received the Purple Heart plus other ribbons.

Marjorie Kunkel, Kittery

Carlton E. Hutchins

Maine citizens proudly remember the gallantry of loved ones participating in this assault:

My father, Stephen Davis, served in the Army 5th Infantry Division. He hit <u>Normandy</u> in the 2nd wave. He received the Bronze Star Infantry Badge, but most of all I was proud to call him my father.

Mark Davis, Rumford
Served during Vietnam era

Stephen Davis

My uncle, Nicholas DeCostanza, served in the U.S. Army from 1943-45. I will honor him by wearing this pin on the days prior to Election Day, on Election Day, and on future election days. He was involved in <u>D-Day</u>…and suffered from what was then called "shell shock." While his war time suffering has passed, his pride in our country lives on.

Kimberly Bowers, Fairfield

My husband, Armand F. Landry, is 100% veteran. He served in the Army for 4 years as a tank driver, from <u>D-Day</u> all the way to Germany, and fought in many battles, too numerous to mention.

Charlotte L. Landry, Sabattus

T. Sgt. Sherman W. Hallowell, Jr. flew 35 missions over the European Theater in WWII. He earned the Distinguished Flying Cross with Three Oak Leaf Clusters, the Air Medal, a Presidential Citation, and two Bronze Stars signifying his participation in <u>D-Day</u> battles. Sherm is truly one of the members of Tom Brokaw's "greatest generation."

Raymond Daniel Spencer, No. Berwick

My dad, Guy F. Donohue, was in the U.S. Army and was in the third wave at Normandy. He supplied fuel for General Patton's Third Army. He was also an interpreter and could ask the farmers, in French, if there were any Germans. He is 77 years old. He is a busy and active man. He looks young for his age. He had 6 children…and I love him to pieces.

Carol A. Proteau, Lewiston

Guy F. Donohue

Guy F. Donohue with man and children in England, 1943.

Guy F. Donohue

Veterans from Maine did not escape the most gruesome horrors of this war:

My brother, Cpl. Guido Oddi, was one of the GIs who helped in the liberation of Dachau Concentration Camp in 1945. He served in the 42nd Infantry Division, U.S. Army.

John A. Oddi, Portland
Served in Infantry in WWII

Memories: Guido Oddi, above left, of Cohasset, helped rescue Steven Ross, right, from Dachau.

I served in the U.S. Army, 45th Division, 180th Infantry from 1944-46 in France and Germany. As a scout, I had to cross our lines and the German lines at night to find out what the Germans were doing and what their moves were, to find out anything and go back through these lines again, most always under fire, and get back to report to my sergeant. My life was only worth 3 seconds. I have the Bronze Star Medal and the Presidential Citation and other medals.

I was also a liberator of Dachau Concentration Camp. I still keep in touch with one of the survivors, Gerda Haas, who has written several books about the holocaust.

Our outfit lost 63,000 men there. I must say the war left me with a lot of nightmares and to this day I have to watch everyone around me and every airplane, wherever it is.

Keith U. Waning

Keith U. Waning, Hollis
Served in 45th Division, 180th Infantry in U.S. Army

My husband, Edward C. Bikulcius, served with the 106th Infantry Division in the Ardennes. He was in Stalag IX-B POW camp and was subjected to forced marches and labor.

Mariette Bikulcius, Lewiston

Edward C. Bikulcius

I am voting in honor of William Helm. He served in the U.S. Army and was a POW held in Germany for months. He has written a paperback book detailing his ordeal, *From the Kennebec to the Elbe River.*

Pam Beaulieu, Wells

I am proud to be voting for Walter Hustus, who served in WWII and was a POW. I am not related to him but knew him well as a resident of Pownal. He died last year.

Sherry Dietrich, Pownal

Walter Hustus

Fall, 1944

The Allied forces under Eisenhower succeed in establishing a front from the North Sea to Switzerland following their invasion in Normandy in June. The Allied forces are stretched very thin.

Hitler thinks a well-executed strike could severely hurt the Allied push towards Germany and possibly turn the tide of the war. He announces plans for an offensive operation, with Antwerp as the objective. **The Ardennes** was the location for the offensive because it offered great cover for massing the necessary forces in secrecy for a surprise German attack.

Dwight David Eisenhower (1890-1969)

*Maine veterans' service included duty in the **Ardennes Forest**:*

My father, U.S. Army Private Gerard P. Jalbert, was an infantryman from the U.S. Army's 9th Division that fought in the African campaign and assaulted Hitler's fortress in Europe, landing in Italy and fighting their way to Germany. His unit saw some of the fiercest hand-to-hand combat of the war and was assigned to a quiet spot in the <u>Ardennes Forest</u> to rest. Unfortunately, this was the heart of the location that Hitler had chosen to counterattack in what came to be known as the Battle of the Bulge. Nearly every man in his unit was killed in the surprise attack, but he had been spared a few days before when American Army officials came through looking for French speakers to act as interpreters. He found the assignment intriguing, a decision that undoubtedly saved his life.

Kathleen Jalbert-Remal, Freeport

I am voting in honor of my father, Laureat J. Lajoie, who served from August 8, 1941 to October 3, 1945. He participated in the battles and campaigns in Normandy, northern France, the Rhineland and <u>the Ardennes</u>. He was a member of Company B, 50th Armored Infantry Battalion, 6th Armored Division as a rifleman. He passed away on April 30, 1974 and is resting in the Maine Veterans Cemetery.

Michelle J. Lajoie, Lewiston

Laureat J. Lajoie

*Soldiers trudging through the snowy **Ardennes Forest**.*

Battle of the Bulge – December 16, 1944

The Battle of the Bulge lasted from December 16, 1944 to January 28, 1945. It was the largest land battle of WWII in which the United States participated. More than a million men fought in this battle including some 600,000 Germans, 500,000 Americans, and 55,000 British. At the conclusion of the battle, the casualties were as follows: 81,000 Americans with 19,000 killed; 1,400 British with 200 killed, and 100,000 Germans killed, wounded or captured.

There had been a race between the 5th Panzer and the American 101st Airborne division to get to Bastogne first and hold it. The Americans won, but by December 25th, the Germans had surrounded the city and moved on.

Bastogne would become the heroic pocket of American resistance to the German offensive, and would be the object of General Patton's amazing counterattack against the German southern flank.

Postcard from General George S. Patton Memorial Museum (California) provided by Mike Burns, Augusta.

"General George S. Patton Jr. was one of the ablest and most controversial U.S. commanders in World War II…Patton distinguished himself in various campaigns including the invasion of North Africa and the capture of Sicily…Patton's expertise in tank command helped frustrate the December 1944 German counteroffensive in the Ardennes at the Battle of the Bulge. Under his command the Third Army swept into Germany and into Czechoslovakia."

For more information about "The American Experience," please visit www.pbs.org/wgbh/amex/.

Several respondents highlighted veterans' connections to **General Patton**:

Patton in jeep aptly titled "War Eagle" inspects units of the 301st Combat Team at Strakonice, Czechoslovakia. Photo taken a short time after General Patton returned to the European Theater.

My dad, August Armelin, worked on Patton's jeep.

Robert M. Armelin, Rockland

My brother, Clyde Parker, served with the 4th Armored Division in the 3rd Army with Patton. He went from the beaches to the outside of Berlin. We are very proud of him.

Paul R. Parker, Norway

I will be voting in honor of my uncle, Aurio Pierro, who served in the U.S. Tank Group. He received 2 Silver Stars as a tank commander and a Purple Heart. He fought in the Battle of the Bulge with General Patton and received the "Unsung Hero Award." He does not talk about it.

Walter Cook, Ogunquit

My uncle, Carl Pulsifer, drove the Jeep for General Patton. He is a hero to me.

Harold D. Gary, Sr., Bucksport
Served in the Navy in Vietnam, 1964-71

I pay tribute to my friend Keith L. Grover. Keith and I grew up together, went to school and college together, enlisted and got our commissions and we both served as officers in the same division in Europe in WWII with General Patton. Keith was KIA, and I was taken POW.

Henry G. Leonard, Norway
Served in WWII

Keith L. Grover

*Voters praise the contributions of veterans who saw action during the **Battle of the Bulge**:*

My father, Major Frederic C. Wall, was a prisoner of war when I was born. He was captured at the <u>Battle of the Bulge</u>.

Frederic C. Wall III, Satsuma, AL

I am voting in honor of my two brothers. Louis Edward Cunningham was a Private in the U.S. Army during WWII. According to his records, he entered military service on March 9, 1943 and was assigned to 106th Reconnaissance Troop, 106th Infantry Division. He fought in the <u>Battle of the Bulge</u> and was captured on December 17, 1944. He was liberated by the British on April 27, 1945 and returned to the states in June. When he was discharged in December of 1945, he had attained the rank of Staff Sergeant. He passed away in 1976.

Louis E. Cunningham

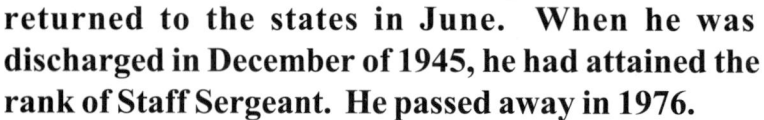

Francis H. Cunningham

My other brother, Francis Herbert Cunningham, also served in the Army during WWII but I do not have his records. Like all veterans, he put his life on the line for our freedom.

Irene C. Estabrook, Bangor

My father, Col. Leslie H. Leighton, M.D., was a medical doctor serving as a Colonel in the U.S. Army during WWII. He participated in the Invasion of Normandy heading up evacuation hospitals throughout the many campaigns in which he was involved. He spent the duration in Europe in various areas, and was an active participant in the <u>Battle of the Bulge</u>. He was an extremely dedicated man, loved and was very proud to be part of the military service. I will wear the button proudly on Election Day in honor of my dad, and the button will be added to the collection of memorabilia in his name that I have documented and keep in memory of his service to his country.

Frances L. Wade, South Casco

At 84, my father, Carlton H. Broadbent, is a WWII veteran who survived being caught behind the lines during the <u>Battle of the Bulge</u>.

Richard C. Broadbent, York

I am voting in honor of my uncle, Joseph Gopan, U.S. Army Ranger. He was a gentleman and hero, but never told war stories…he was captured leading a patrol during the <u>Battle of Bulge</u>. He returned to Bangor and became a respected business leader. I have a museum-quality Jeep and Army truck with his unit markings on it to honor him.

1941 GMC 2½ ton Army truck

Joel Gopan, Hampden

Leo K. Lick

When I vote, I will pay tribute to Leo K. Lick, who received the Silver Star and Bronze Star. He fought in the Sicilian campaign, the Invasion of Normandy, and the <u>Battle of the Bulge</u>. I was his platoon sergeant. He was a real all-around good person and an outstanding soldier. He now lives in Gaylord, Minnesota.

George W. Eldridge, North Berwick
Served in 1st Infantry Division in Africa, Sicily, and Normandy

Battle of the Hedgerows

Germans believe that these battles on the beaches are only diversionary tactics, so they do little to organize sizable counterattacks on D-Day. Allied aircraft and French resistance fighters impede the movement of German reserves, but the Germans are able to defend terrain in the French countryside known as "hedgerow country." High banks of earth around every small field had been erected to fence livestock and protect crops. The Germans turned each field into a small fortress.

The Third U.S. Army under General Patton enters the line to end the battle of the hedgerows. Through a variety of successful Allied maneuvers, the German forces begin to withdraw. The men and women of the French resistance battle the Germans in the streets of Paris. The German forces fall back in defeat toward the German frontier.

The Final Allied Assaults

Early in 1945, while U.S. troops continue their drive in southern France, Soviet armies start a drive toward the Oder River, only 40 miles from Berlin. The Germans have little chance of holding west of the Rhine. General Eisenhower continues the U.S. push through central Germany to link with the Russians.

By mid-April Allied armies make contact with the Red Army approaching from the east. Berlin falls to the Soviets. Hitler commits suicide. German troops surrender all along the German front and in Italy.

War in Europe is Over

On May 7, 1945, the German Government surrenders. **May 8, 1945** is V-E Day, Victory in Europe…and the end of the war in Europe.

V-E Day, May 8, 1945

> The Allied forces in Western Europe totaled 4 1/2 million military personnel. The Allies had 28,000 combat aircraft, and they had brought into Western Europe more than 970,000 vehicles and 18 million tons of supplies.

More Tributes to Veterans' Patriotism and Loyalty

*Of all the responses received for the **Vote in Honor of a Veteran** program, nearly half of them honored servicemen and women who served during World War II. The following represent some of the heartfelt tributes to the courage, commitment, and honor of veterans during this unparalleled chapter in world history:*

I am voting in honor of Francis Gagnon, aka "Hawk Canyon," who is a disabled WWII Army veteran and a strong, outspoken advocate for veterans' rights. He passed away a few years ago, but he was a fighter to the end.

Douglas J. Ward, Sanford
Served in Cuba, Vietnam, and Grenada
USAF (Ret.)

I want to pay tribute to my uncle, Harold Stevenson, who served in the Army. He was left on the battlefield for dead but a soldier from Bangor saved his life.

Roberta Alls, Hampden

Harold Stevenson - left

I am voting in honor of my grandfather, Reginald R. Boober, Sr., who served in WWII. Every day my grandfather is missed more and more…he passed away February 12, 1998.

Susan M. Boober, Bangor

When I vote, I will do so in honor of my father, Richard Adams. He won the Purple Heart for his service in the European Theater and was active in American Legion and VFW. He passed on the principles of loyalty and patriotism to all of his children and grandchildren.

"Dad passed away on October 20th, and never got to vote this year, a duty that he took very seriously. This opportunity to remember him will mean a lot to our family."

Kathy Adams-Iller, Auburn

I am proud of the service of my grandfather, Alden Tracy, Sr. who was a Staff Sergeant in the Army during WWII. He helped build the Panama Canal.

Jennifer Abbott, Ellsworth

Alden Tracy, Sr.

Alden Tracy, Sr.

I am voting in honor of my father, Chester M. Greczkowski, Sr. My father misrepresented his age to join the Army – he was only 15. He was wounded twice and received 2 Purple Hearts and numerous other decorations. He is the father of 12 children, grandfather to 34, and great-grandfather to 6.

Brenda K. Adler, Gray

I will be voting proudly in remembrance of my friend, Laura Geddes, a commander in the U.S. Navy in WWII. She died this year at the age of 101 and was a pioneer in many ways during her whole life.

Margaret M. Sheridan, Monroe

Laura Geddes

Laura Geddes

When I vote, I will be remembering all my buddies who died. They were the greatest bunch of men and women that ever lived.

Clayton F. Teague, Freeport
Served from 1942-45, 3 years in the Army Air Force and 1 year in the Infantry

I am proud of my grandfather, Victor Willette, who served his country faithfully and honorably in the Army during WWII.

Ken Oiler, Costigan
Served in Army National Guard in Bosnia & Grenada

Victor Willette

I pay tribute to my twin sister, Dorothy Patt Perlgut, who was a WAVE in WWII. She served as a Storekeeper 1st class in Virginia and Georgia.

Selma Shure, Searsmont

The Nuremberg Trials – At the close of the war, four countries – the United States, Great Britain, France, and the Soviet Union – signed an agreement that perpetrators would be tried for war crimes. The Nuremberg Trials were conducted between October 20, 1945 and October 1, 1946.

I am voting in honor of my father, Lawrence Andersen, who was wounded in Germany. He served as an interpreter at the Nuremberg Trials because he was able to translate in both French and German.

Rachel Seymour, Old Town

I am voting in honor of my brother, Floyd M. Elwell, Jr., who served in the U.S. Army at the close of WWII and was the head chef for the German prisoners during the Nuremberg Trials. We served together with another brother, Richard, in Vietnam from 1965-66. Floyd died in November 1999.

Floyd M. Elwell, Jr.

Richard, Freddie and Floyd Elwell

Frederick W. Elwell, SFC (Ret.), Bath
Served in U.S. Army in Vietnam

Chapter 3

1945-1990: THE COLD WAR ERA

Korean Conflict (1950-1953)
"America's Forgotten War"

"Duty. Honor. Country. Those three hallowed words reverently dictate what you ought to be, what you can be, what you will be. They are your rallying point to build courage when courage seems to fail, to regain faith when there seems to be little cause for faith, to create hope when hope becomes forlorn."

General Douglas MacArthur (1880 – 1964)
Address to the cadets of the U.S. Military Academy in accepting the Thayer Award May 12, 1962

—U.S. Army Truman Museum & Library photo

The Cold War

The end of World War II left the United States and the USSR the two greatest powers in the world. However, by 1947, friction over the treaties with Austria, Germany, and Japan and Soviet aggression in Eastern Europe brought increasing tension. By the end of 1948, the relationship between the United States and the Soviet Union was considered a **cold war.**

After World War II the Korean peninsula, about the size of the state of Utah, extending 635 miles in length and 150 miles across at its widest, had been divided along the 38th parallel into South Korea and North Korea. The South declared itself the Republic of Korea and the North, the Democratic People's Republic of Korea.

In 1950, armed conflict arose in Korea between Soviet-backed Communist forces and United Nations forces led by the United States. U.S. policymakers were committed to extending the Truman Doctrine, which called for the containment of Communism in southeast Asia.

June 25, 1950 – North Korea invades South Korea along the line of demarcation. This action marks the beginning of the conflict, eventually called the Korean Conflict. Secretary of State Dean Acheson and President Truman are persuaded to commit air and naval power to the region and to deploy the 7th Fleet to the Taiwan Strait to prevent mainland China from invading the island of Taiwan. In all, fifteen nations, in addition to the United States, send combat troops to fight in Korea.

Mainers proudly voted in honor of loved ones who served in Korea:

My husband, Benjamin W. Barr, Sr., served in the U.S. Air Force during the Korean Conflict. He believed in freedom for everyone. He loved his country and our flag. I have listened to my husband talk of the war and watched the tears fall down his face. But when I asked him and my uncles who served in World War II and Korea why they went in to the service, their answer was simply, "So our brothers, sisters and our children to come wouldn't have to go." They gave so much so we would be free and safe.

Janice A. Barr, Medway

My father, Benjamin W. Barr, Sr., served in the Korean Conflict. Although he was not an honored hero in a military way, he will always be my hero. Also, his dedication to veterans, their families, and our community is an honor in itself. He loved his country, the State of Maine, and veterans in general. At his memorial service a gentleman said it about as well as anyone possibly could: "I feel I am standing in the shadow of a very great man." Indeed sir, you were.

Kimberly M. Lyons, Lincoln

I am voting in honor of my brother, William J. Champlin, who served in the Army in Korea. He helped lead 7 men to safety from behind enemy lines.

Francis T. Champlin, Van Buren
Served from 1957-1961

I will vote in honor of my husband, Petty Officer, 2nd class, Paul Joseph Pepin, who served in the Navy for four years during the Korean Conflict. He served aboard the battleship *New Jersey* and took part in ship to shore bombardments, making it safer for the ground crews to do their jobs. He was the recipient of three battle stars and the Korean Presidential Unit of Citation, among others. I am very proud of him and the positive attitude he has regarding the defense of our great country.

Paul Joseph Pepin

Joyce H. Pepin, Newport

Deanna & Elmer "Bud" Hallett

When I vote, I will do so with pride in honor of my husband, Elmer "Bud" Hallett, who served with honor in the U.S. Navy during the Korean Conflict. He was in the hospital on Election Day 2000, but I was pleased to be able to acknowledge his service time and to give a very sick man a smile. He died November 19 and is sadly missed.

Deanna Mosher Hallett, Hallowell

Charles M. Johnson

C Co. 1st Bn 6th Marines 2nd Div.

My father, Charles M. Johnson, was a staff sergeant in the Marine Corps and served 5 years in the service. He was in the Korean Conflict and was wounded twice. He received a Bronze Star, 2 Purple Hearts, and other medals. I am very proud of him.

Gary C. Johnson, Sr., Fairfield

My father, Jerry L. DeWitt, turned 18 while he was in Korea. He was a Ranger. My mother, Sharon H. Howard, served in the Airborne Women's Army Corps.

Hans D. DeWitt, Wilton

Some of the most well known battles of the Korean Conflict were the several battles for **Pork Chop Hill, Old Baldy,** *and* **Heartbreak Ridge***:*

My father, Edward Ouellet, enlisted in the U.S. Army in April of 1952, leaving home with high ideals and a strong sense of duty for his country. After he was wounded at <u>Pork Chop Hill</u>, he spent over 4 months in a hospital in Japan and received a Purple Heart. When he returned home, he married and raised 4 children. My father shared with us his beliefs of patriotism. He motivated us with encouragement to serve our country. Where we come from and from whom we come determines our character. I am proud to be my father's daughter. I am proud of the veteran who raised me.

Edward Ouellet

Brenda Boyce, Ashland

I will be proudly wearing the veteran button in honor of my father, Jesse R. Wilson, who fought in the Korean Conflict with the United States Army's 180th Infantry Regiment and 45th Infantry Division on <u>Old Baldy</u>. After ten months of being on the front lines, my dad was hit by a mortar and wounded in the right leg. He was given the Purple Heart for shedding his blood for the freedom of our country. I am very thankful for the sacrifices he made and that he is alive today to tell me about them.

Debra L. Wilson, Old Town

I am voting in honor of Cpl. Fred C. Berry, Jr., a native of Brunswick, who died on June 27, 1951. We were behind enemy lines, flushing out the enemy. Suddenly we were fired on by a 2-machine gun nest on high ground. Fred turned and attacked, firing as he went. He cleaned out gun No. 1 and started for gun No. 2. He was almost there when a grenade got him. He was awarded the Silver Star posthumously.

Joseph W. Boulet, Sanford
Served in Korea, 1951

Fred C. Berry, Jr.

Compelling responses honoring veterans of the Korean Conflict recalled those who unselfishly and valiantly gave their lives in service to their country, some at particularly young ages:

My brother, PFC Donald G. Feeney, served in the 1st Marine Division in the Korean Conflict. He died on November 9, 1950, with only a few weeks left to serve. He was only 20 years old.

Evelyn J. (Feeney) Cave, Orrington

My brother, Cpl. George Riley Burton, served in Korea in the 15th Field Battalion, 2nd Infantry Division, Army. He died in a North Korean prison camp of wounds and beriberi. He was 18 years old.

Hilda E. Thibodeau, Veazie

George Riley Burton

My father, Captain Roger W. Jellison, was an Air Force pilot killed in action in 1957. I am also voting in honor of my mother, Jo Doris Jellison, who was an active duty registered nurse in the USAF from 1948-1956.

Michael Jellison, Hampden

I am voting in honor of my uncle, Kenneth Wayne Merrill, who served in the Army. According to a letter sent to the family, "A Chinese mortar round killed him as he almost single-handedly held off an enemy regiment on June 3, 1953." He was only 19 years old. He was very proud to serve his country. He received the Silver Star, the Bronze Star, and the Purple Heart, among other citations.

Donnalene MacDonald, Casco

Kenneth Wayne Merrill

My cousin, Harry L. Sargent, Jr., was in the Army in the tank division when he was killed during the Korean Conflict. He is buried on a knoll overlooking the Korean War Memorial with his name etched in granite in the Hope Cemetery in Bangor. He was the only child of Harry and Emily Sargent of Hampden.

Judith C. Mosier, Yarmouth

I will be voting in honor of John Hickey, who served in the Air Force in the Korean Conflict. He was shot down and died in a POW camp. He was the only one from Maine that I met over there. This is for John Hickey and all the others on the Korean War Memorial in Bangor.

Carl A. Leighton, Princeton
Served in Korean Conflict, 1951-52

When I vote, I will pay tribute to my brother, Cpl. Irving Munroe, who was a member of a B-29 bomber squad flying without fighter escort deep in North Korea. They were attacked by large numbers of North Korean jet fighters and shot down. On 1 June 1951 he became MIA. He was 19 years old.

Jack J. Munroe, Stetson
Served in Korea and Vietnam, U.S. Army Ret.

MAINE KOREAN WAR MEMORIAL

The Maine Korean War Memorial was dedicated July 29, 1995, two days after the national memorial was dedicated in Washington, D.C.

It is located on a beautiful site next to a tranquil pond in Mt. Hope Cemetery, Bangor, Maine, and it salutes all veterans of the first United Nations action since the end of the Second World War.

The memorial reflects the work of a small group of Korean War Veterans who began in 1992 to plan how to construct an appropriate memorial to the Korean War honoring all Maine servicemen and women, especially those who were killed in Korea.

On polished granite slabs are engraved the names of 233 Maine men who died in Korea. Eight additional names are to be added as a result of further investigations. The memorial also provides visitors with a history lesson about the "Forgotten War".

I will be voting in honor of Roy Sandvik, United States Marines. He was killed in action in Korea. He was one of my best friends.

Kenneth Carlsen, Brooklyn, NY
Served in Korea, USMC

I will be voting in honor of my uncle, Glendon Philbrick, who was killed in the Korean Conflict serving in the Army for our freedom. He died 3 days before the war was over.

Tina Marie Richard, Clinton

Glendon Philbrick

I will be voting in honor of Joe Mahoney, USMC, my first buddy killed in Korea.

Richard G. Chick, Winthrop
Served in Korea

Equally touching are responses that honor the sacrifice, patriotism, and dedication of loved ones who did their duty abroad and then came home:

My grandfather, Kenneth L. Hall, Sr., was in the Navy during the Korean Conflict. He was a gunner's mate on a ship. While he was serving, he contracted pneumatic fever and was sent home. He and my grandmother were married for 45 years before he passed away in 1995. I would like to vote in his memory and in honor of a time in his life of which he was very proud but spoke little.

Jennifer M. Bassett, Auburn

I will vote in honor of my wife, Shirley Ayer Lupo, who joined the Navy in 1952 but was required to be discharged in 1955 because she got married. (At that time if a female married, she had to leave the military.) Her most interesting flight was in 1954 when she took French troops from Indo-China back to Paris.

Raymond R. Lupo, Hampden
Served 5 years in the Navy and 15 years
in the Air Force in Korea, Vietnam and the Congo

My father, Frank William McDade, fought in Korea. I am proud that he helped secure the freedom we now hold so dear. This is a great way to honor him.

Earl Matthew McDade, Bangor

Frank William McDade

Army Nurse Corps personnel serving in Korea followed time-honored traditions in accepting the challenging responsibilities of combat nursing. They managed over-whelming numbers of critically wounded soldiers in MASH (Mobile Army Surgical Hospital) units, in Field Hospitals, and Evacuation Hospitals.

The exact number of Army Nurse Corps officers who saw action in the Korean Conflict is unknown; estimates of nurse participants vary from 540 to 1,502.

The **Air Force Nurse Corps** assisted in the evacuation of about 3,900 patients after the Chinese intervention in the war. By the end of the war, they had helped evacuate about 350,000 patients.

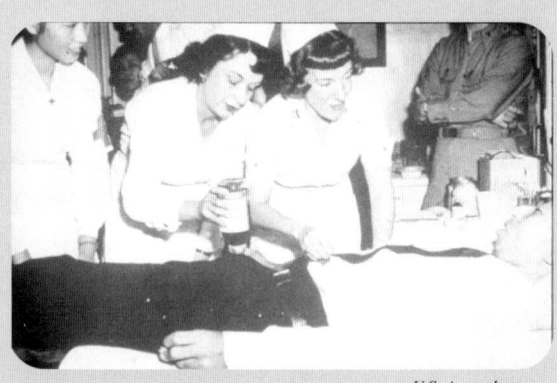

—*U.S. Army photo*

The **Navy Nurse Corps** served in hospitals as well as aboard ships where battle casualties were admitted. Hospital ships were a new type of mobile hospital moving from place to place, supporting invasions, aiding evacuations, or staying near the coast as needed.

I am voting in honor of my companion, Jeannie Harrington, who was a CT in the Navy in the early 50's and served as a reservist on active duty. She was the founder of WAVES National with a unit in Maine.

Ralph Dicks, Milo

Jeannie Harrington

My son, Russell Lane Jr., served his country in the Army in Korea. I'm proud he served. Everyone should. It would be a better place to live.

Russell Lane, Sr., Bristol

My brother, Vaughan L. Tardiff, is the oldest of 12 children, 9 boys and 3 girls. Vaughan served in Korea. All the rest of the brothers also served in the military for a total of <u>106 years</u>.

Gerald E. Tardiff, Brewer
Served in Vietnam, USMC (Ret.)

When I vote, I will be paying tribute to my husband, Sylvio L. Thibodeau, a veteran who served in Korea. He is a very active V.F.W. member. He puts up 16 flags in our town on each holiday when flags are designated to be flown.

Lucille F. Thibodeau, Lee

Sylvio L. Thibodeau

I am voting in honor of Cornelius J. Begin, Jr., my husband, who served in the U.S. Navy from 1951 - 1955 aboard the *USS Wasp*. He was honorably discharged in 1955.

Dorothy L. Begin, Winslow

Cornelius J. Begin, Jr.

It was the patriotism of my father, Cornelius J. Begin, Jr., and his love for his country that encouraged me to join the Navy thirty years later.

Donna J. Fenton, Vassalboro
Served in U.S. Navy from 1981-86

My brother, Norman O'Clair, served our country in the Army during the Korean Conflict. He was the sole survivor of a landslide and was seriously injured. He is now 71 years old. I admire his bravery and sacrifice. He is the oldest of fourteen children and I am the youngest. He got news of my birth while on a hospital ship on his way back home to the states. Another brother, Paul, wanted to be with Norman in Korea and lied about his age to join the Army. He was on his way to Korea the same time Norman was on his way back home.

Norman O'Clair

Catherine Herson, Sorrento

I am voting in honor of my husband, William R. Gilbert, who served in the Army in Korea from 1956-1958.

Alice M. Gilbert, Fairfield

William R. Gilbert

Aftermath of the Korean Conflict

The United States, North Korea and China signed an armistice. However, the agreement failed to bring about a permanent peace.

U.S. forces had not previously seen a conflict like Korea. The battles were hard-fought, the enemy was unpredictable, and the weather was extreme. Over 1.7 million Americans served in Korea. Estimates are that more than 33,000 service members died. There were over 103,000 casualties and 7,140 military personnel taken as prisoners of war.

MEDALS OF HONOR

There were 131 Medals of Honor awarded to U.S. servicemen for their actions during the Korean Conflict. Three Medals of Honor were given to veterans from Maine.

Army *Navy*  *Air Force*

Major Charles J. Loring "The last Air Force Medal of Honor was awarded posthumously to *Major Charles J. Loring Jr.* Loring was an F-80 pilot and flight leader assigned to the 80th Fighter-Bomber Squadron. On November 22, 1952, he led a quartet of F-80's against enemy artillery emplacements on Sniper Ridge which were harassing friendly ground troops. After verifying his target, Loring began his bombing run. Enemy fire was extremely heavy and accurate throughout his dive and his aircraft was hit and crippled.

Disdaining any attempt to head for safety, Loring pulled up in a deliberate and controlled maneuver. He then turned and dove into a group of active gun emplacements, destroying them.

Major Charles J. Loring

In a ceremony in the White House held on May 5, 1954, President Dwight D. Eisenhower presented the Medal of Honor to Loring's widow.

On October 1, 1954, Limestone Air Force Base, Maine, was renamed *Loring Air Force Base* in his honor."

—from The Archives of the *Portland Press Herald*

Corporal Clair Goodblood, of Fort Kent, served in the U.S. Army, Company D, 7th Infantry Regiment during the Korean Conflict.

According to his Medal of Honor Citation:
"Corporal Goodblood distinguished himself by conspicuous gallantry and intrepidity at the risk of his life above and beyond the call of duty in action against an armed enemy of the United Nations on 24 and 25 April 1951 near Popsu-dong, Korea. Corporal Goodblood, a machine gunner, was attached to Company B in defensive positions on thickly wooded key terrain under attack by a ruthless foe. In bitter fighting which ensued, the numerically superior enemy infiltrated the perimeter, rendering the friendly positions untenable. Upon order to move back, Corporal Goodblood voluntarily remained to cover the withdrawal and, constantly vulnerable to heavy fire, inflicted withering destruction on the assaulting force... He fearlessly maintained his one-man defense, sweeping the onrushing assailants with fire until an enemy banzai charge carried the hill and silenced his gun. When friendly elements regained the commanding ground, Corporal Goodblood's body was found lying beside his gun and approximately 100 hostile dead lay in the wake of his field of fire. Through his unflinching courage and willing self-sacrifice the onslaught was retarded, enabling his unit to withdraw, regroup and resecure the strongpoint. Corporal Goodblood's inspirational conduct and devotion to duty reflect lasting glory on himself and are in keeping with the noble traditions of the military service."

Captain Lewis L. Millett, of Mechanic Falls, served in the U.S. Army, Company E, 27th Infantry Regiment, during the Korean Conflict.

According to his Medal of Honor Citation:
"Captain Millett distinguished himself by conspicuous gallantry and intrepidity above and beyond the call of duty in action in the vicinity of Soam-Ni, Korea on February 7, 1951. While personally leading his company in an attack against a strongly held position he noted that the 1st platoon was pinned down by small-arms, automatic, and antitank fire. Captain Millett ordered the 3rd platoon forward, placed himself at the head of the two platoons, and, with fixed bayonet, led the assault up the fire-swept hill... His dauntless leadership and personal courage so inspired his men that they stormed into the hostile position and used their bayonets with such lethal effect that the enemy fled in wild disorder. During this onslaught Captain Millett was wounded by grenade fragments but refused evacuation until the objective was taken and firmly secured. The superb leadership, conspicuous courage, and consummate devotion to duty demonstrated by Captain Millett were directly responsible for the successful accomplishment of a hazardous mission and reflect the highest credit on himself and the heroic traditions of the military service."

*Colonel (Ret.) Lewis L. Millett, one of the four surviving Maine Medal of Honor recipients, currently resides in Idyllwild, California

*from **United States of America's Congressional Medal of Honor Recipients and Their Official Citations,** provided by the Office of the Adjutant General, State of Maine*

Special Citations Given to Two Medal of Honor Recipients Born in Maine

Corporal David B. Champagne, entered the service in Rhode Island but was born in Waterville, Maine, and served in U.S. Marine Corps, Company A, 1st Battalion, 7th Marines, 1st Marine Division, in Korea. On 28 May 1952, "Cpl. Champagne, by his valiant leadership, fortitude, and gallant spirit of self-sacrifice in the face of almost certain death, undoubtedly saved the lives of several of his fellow Marines. His heroic actions served to inspire all who observed him and reflected the highest credit upon himself and the U.S. Naval Service. He gallantly gave his life for his country."

Sergeant George D. Libby, entered the service in Connecticut but was born in Bridgton, Maine, and served in the U.S. Army, Company C, 3rd Engineer Combat Battalion, 24th Infantry Division, near Taejon, Korea. On 20 July 1950, Sgt. Libby's "sustained, heroic actions enabled his comrades to reach friendly lines. His dauntless courage and gallant self-sacrifice reflect the highest credit upon himself and uphold the esteemed traditions of the U.S. Army."

from ***United States of America's Congressional Medal of Honor Recipients and Their Official Citations,*** *provided by the Office of the Adjutant General, State of Maine*

Vietnam Conflict (1961-1975)

"They say:
  Our deaths are not ours;
  they are yours;
  they will mean what
    you make them."

from the poem **"The Young Dead Soldiers"** by **Archibald MacLeish** (1892-1982)

- from *Collected Poems, 1917-1982* by Archibald MacLeish. Copyright 1985 by the Estate of Archibald MacLeish. Reprinted by permission of Houghton Mifflin Company. All rights reserved.

Prelude to the War: 1954-1960

The Battle of Dien Bien Phu between Vietnamese forces and the French in 1954 lasted 55 days. Three thousand French troops were killed, 8,000 wounded. The Viet Minh suffered 8,000 deaths and 12,000 personnel were wounded.

This battle is considered by many historians to be a defining moment in Southeast Asia.

During 1959 a specialized North Vietnamese Army unit is formed to create a supply route from North Vietnam to Vietcong forces in South Vietnam. This primitive route along the Vietnamese/Cambodian border eventually becomes known as the Ho Chi Minh Trail.

The U.S. Steps Up Involvement

1961 – President Kennedy orders more help for the South Vietnamese government in its war against the Vietcong guerillas. More than 3,000 military advisors and support personnel are sent.

1962 – Helicopters flown by U.S. Army pilots mark the first U.S. combat missions against the Vietcong.

Maine voters wrote about military service in Vietnam and the challenges of helicopter duty:

I am voting in honor of James Godfrey, a boyhood friend and schoolmate. He joined the Army and became a helicopter pilot. He was killed in Vietnam.

Robert D. Hodgkins, Greene
Served in Vietnam and Desert Storm

My Army buddy, James Franklin, was a fixed wing and chopper pilot in Vietnam.

Richard E. Giffard, Brewer
U.S. Army (Ret.), served in Korea and Vietnam

James Franklin

Vast tracks of forest are sprayed with "Agent Orange," an herbicide containing the deadly chemical Dioxin. Guerilla trails are exposed and crops that might feed Vietcong are destroyed.

I am voting in honor of my son, Mark A. Michaud, who received the following Award of the Air Medal for Heroism:

Mark A. Michaud

"While participating in aerial flight in the Republic of Vietnam, Specialist Four Mark A. Michaud distinguished himself as a crew chief of a UH-1H helicopter. When his aircraft became the target of intense enemy automatic weapons fire, Specialist Michaud continuously exposed himself to the enemy while providing suppressive fire. After the aircraft was rendered unflyable, and he was saturated with aviation fuel from the leaking fuel cells, he continued to suppress the enemy with intense machine-gun fire...Specialist Michaud's heroic actions were in keeping with the highest traditions of the military service and reflect great credit upon himself, his unit, and the United States Army."

He died on June 29, 2000 at 52 years of age from the effects of Agent Orange.

Lawrence A. Michaud, Ashland

1963-1964 – The Vietcong and local guerillas ambush the South Vietnamese on January 2, 1963.

Almost 400 South Vietnamese are killed or wounded.

On **November 22, 1963**, President John F. Kennedy is assasinated. Vice President Lyndon Baines Johnson becomes President.

Lyndon Baines Johnson
36th President of the United States

At this time 16,000 military advisors are in Vietnam. The Kennedy administration had run the war from Washington without large-scale commitment of American combat troops.

President Johnson, however, argues for more expansive war powers after the raid on two U.S. ships in the Gulf of Tonkin.

April-June 1964 – American air power is massively reinforced and two aircraft carriers arrive off the Vietnamese coast prompted by a North Vietnamese offensive in Laos.

Early August, 1964 – Forces of the Democratic Republic of Vietnam (DRV) attack two American ships in the Gulf of Tonkin.

August 7, 1964 – The U.S. Congress passes the Gulf of Tonkin Resolution, giving President Johnson the power to take whatever actions he deems necessary to defend Southeast Asia.

1965 – President Johnson sends the first combat troops to Vietnam.

1965-1967 – There are not enough volunteers to continue to fight a protracted war and the government institutes a draft.

Sentiment against the U.S. participation in the war increases. Growing numbers of citizens begin to question whether the U.S. effort can succeed, and they express their dissatisfaction in peace marches, demonstrations, and acts of civil disobedience.

This was a period of overwhelming personal losses and dramatic sacrifices:

We pay tribute to father and "Grampie," Richard A. Greene, who served in the Army in Vietnam during 1965-66.

Audrey Greene, Kenduskeag, daughter
Shauni Greene, Kenduskeag, granddaughter

I am voting in honor of Sgt. Charles Benjamin Norris, USMC. I left Vietnam in mid-March of 1966. Sgt. Norris took over my squad but he was killed on 21 April 1966. We had never met.

James N. Phinney, Pittsfield
Served in Vietnam, 1964-66

Born in Waterville, David Walter Marlborough was one of 34 killed June 8, 1967 on the *USS Liberty*. He was the only Maine resident to be killed during this "6-Day War."

Kenneth C. Johnson, Lamoine
Served in Vietnam era

Robert (Bobbie) Blye and I served in Vietnam together. At least once he saved my life. He was killed in action, November 21, 1967.

Frank D. Connors, Bowdoinham
Served in Vietnam

Robert Blye & Frank D. Connors

I am voting in honor of my mom and dad, Rena and Gerard Wynn. Dad was a graduate of West Point, class of 1956. He was a Major and served with the U.S. Army, Special Forces. He died during his 2nd tour of duty in Vietnam in 1967. Mom had met Dad while she was serving as an Army Nurse, 1st Lt.

Elizabeth Wynn Shirk, South Portland

My best friend, Joe Shumpert, was killed in Vietnam in the Army on December 25, 1967. I sure miss him.

Randall C. Ellis, Belfast
Served in Vietnam, 1967-68

My brother, Marvin W. Woodbury, served with the 4th Infantry from 1966-1969. He did two tours so I wouldn't have to go to Vietnam, but I went after he came home.

Donald P. Woodbury, Gorham
Served in Vietnam

1968 The Tet Offensive

Vietnamese tradition held that the turning of the lunar year should bring auspicious signs and gladness of heart; thus, it had become customary for both sides to observe a truce during the holiday celebrations. In 1968, a thirty-six hour cease-fire had been agreed upon, to commence at midnight on January 30.

However, a little after midnight on January 30, Communist-led forces assault the Nra Trang perimeter. All day long… they attacked provincial capitals and divisional headquarters…Vietcong soldiers were fighting in the streets of Hue, DaNang and Saigon itself.

—Vets with a Mission Vietnam Photo Journal of the Tet Offensive

Tet Offensive, January 30, 1968

The **Tet Offensive** brought the war to the cities for the first time. General Westmoreland established **Operation Recovery** to coordinate the rebuilding process for these cities.

Please put the number "37" on my Vote for a Veteran button. This represents the men in my unit who were killed and that I helped to unload from my chopper during <u>Tet</u> in '68.

Willis Stanley, Palmyra
Served in Vietnam, 1967-69

I am honoring my uncle, Cpl. André Dubé, USMC, who was killed during the <u>Tet Offensive</u>. He was the youngest of 13 children and signed up because my father had also served in Vietnam as a Marine. My dad escorted his body home.

Mike Dubé, Madawaska
Served in Grenada, West Indies, Beirut and Lebanon

André Dubé

My brother, André L. Dubé, served in the USMC from June 1963 to August 1966, when he was killed in action. He received his first Purple Heart in March of 1966. He requested to remain in country for his duration. He was 21 years old.

John T. Dubé, Jay
Served in Vietnam, U.S. Navy

André Dubé

I was wounded 3 times in the <u>Tet Offensive</u> in 1968. I served in the 9th Infantry, U.S. Army.

Jerry A. Elwell, Bristol
Served in Vietnam

> By 1968, troop levels had reached 495,000. There had been 30,000 American deaths to date; approximately 1,000 were killed a month.

I volunteered another tour of duty for my buddy Mike Deschaine and will vote in his honor at this Election. Mike and I grew up together in Auburn. He served in the 1st Marine Division and was KIA in his 3rd month in Vietnam.

Bertrand L. Levesque, Lisbon
Did 2 combat tours in Vietnam, 1967-70

I am honoring Dennis Graham, my college friend at Texas A&M College, an all male military school at the time. Dennis was poor, as we all were in this small college. Most of our families were sacrificing to get us through college. I know he worked in the mess hall three meals a day to help pay for his education. He was the one of us who did not drink and also was the Wing Chaplin— just the All-American young man.

We all graduated and went to pilot training. Dennis was my roommate during pilot training. After graduation we went to different planes, I to B-52s and Dennis to the F-111. Dennis told me when he got home he would leave the Air Force and fly for the Texas Air National Guard (F-102). He said the F-111 was a dangerous aircraft because the terrain-following radar had some problems. That was the last time I talked to him.

Six F-111s were sent to fly into Vietnam. They lost 3 in two weeks. Dennis was in the first one, as I understand. He was killed (MIA), an example of the waste of fine young men this war produced, a war this country was not willing to make the hard decisions to win.

Windol C. Weaver, York
USAF, 3 tours in Vietnam

My son, S/Sgt. Wayne C. Cyr, was a great, courageous soldier. He enlisted at age 17. He served in the Army Infantry and was killed in Vietnam on May 7, 1968, barely 21 years old. His brother, Master Sergeant Alvin Cyr made the Army his career and recently retired.

Bernice Maxheimer, Cherryfield

*A variety of requests to **Vote in Honor of a Veteran** were heartfelt memories that fondly recalled the importance of friends and loved ones:*

Cloyce Gress was a good buddy in my unit in Vietnam when we served together from 1968-69. He found me via computer after 30 years of separation.

Randall Grady, Jefferson
Served in Vietnam

Cloyce Gress & Randall Grady
1969

I am voting in honor of my son, George J. Bursey, who was awarded the following Army Commendation Medal for heroism:

"On March 14, 1968, PFC. Bursey was serving as a radio-telephone operator with a forward observer on a reconnaissance in force operation in the vicinity of Cu Chi. His platoon was moving through dense jungle terrain when they were suddenly subjected to intense small arms and automatic weapons fire from a well concealed Viet Cong force...He observed several seriously wounded personnel lying in an area which was exposed to heavy enemy fire and, with complete disregard for his personal safety, immediately ran to their aid and assisted in carrying them to safety. His exemplary courage and initiative were instrumental in saving the lives of several of his fellow soldiers, and significantly contributed to the successful outcome of the encounter."

George E. Bursey, Trenton
Served in WWII

My husband, Gerald L. Caron, served in Vietnam in 1968. He went with the priest to the orphanage on Sundays so he could translate because he spoke French. He loved the children and would gladly have taken one of them home with him if he could have. He is very patriotic. He would go anywhere in the world to protect his family and country.

Claudette Caron, Lewiston

Gerald L. Caron

My father, Manuel Moreno, served in the Army for 23 years and fought in the Vietnam War. He is disabled from the war. I have great respect and appreciation for him.

Janice Moreno, Richmond

I will vote in honor of my brother-in-law, Ken Stowe, of Topsfield, Massachusetts, who served in the army in Vietnam. His job was working with German Shepherds to train them to find land mines. One of his best dogs blew up in front of him on a land mine, saving his life.

Priscilla D. Hoekstra, Etna

1968 - 1972 – During 1969 action in South Vietnam is scattered and limited. In June, President Richard M. Nixon announces the withdrawal of 25,000 U.S. troops. There are more than 540,000 U.S. military personnel in Vietnam.

During spring of 1970 the Ho Chi Minh Trail is the constant target of B-52 bomber raids. Fighting expands into Cambodia, and new waves of anti-war protests erupt in the United States. By late 1970 the number of personnel in South Vietnam is 335,000.

The gradual withdrawal of military personnel in South Vietnam proceeds, but the peace talks are in a stalemate. The South Vietnamese take responsibility for fighting on the ground, but U.S. air support is still needed. The number of military personnel has dropped to 160,000.

In 1972 the North Vietnamese invade the DMZ and capture Quang Tri province. President Nixon responds by ordering intense bombing of the North.

President Richard M. Nixon
37th President of the United States

Maine voters honor veterans who served during this challenging time:

I will be voting in honor of Robert W. Fields. Bob was a medical doctor that I served with in the 14th USAF Hospital, Nha Trang, RVN. He was in a helicopter, which was shot down. He died in the crash on 26 March 1969. He was a good doctor and a good man.

Charlie Smith, Presque Isle
Served in Vietnam

I met Joe Nye when he was in Togus VA Hospital with me. I don't know his real first name – all he ever told me was "Joe." He was one of the most decorated servicemen in Vietnam. He felt strongly that the vets who returned from Desert Storm should be treated like heroes, not like the guys who came home from Vietnam. I really admired him.

Robert B. Chapman, Bangor

I want to honor SFC Yano and all patriots who have made the supreme sacrifice to ensure the torch of freedom will always burn brightly. I never met Sergeant First Class Yano, but this General Order tells all:

"Sergeant First Class Rodney J. T. Yano, United States Army, distinguished himself on 1 January 1969 while serving with the Air Cavalry Troop, 11th Cavalry Regiment, in the vicinity of Bien Hoa, Republic of Vietnam. Sergeant Yano was performing the duties of crew chief aboard the troop's command-and-control helicopter during action against enemy forces entrenched in dense jungle. From an exposed position in the face of intense small arms and antiaircraft fire he delivered suppressive fire upon the enemy forces and marked their positions with smoke and white phosphorous grenades, thus enabling his troop commander to direct accurate and effective artillery fire against the hostile emplacements. A grenade, exploding prematurely, covered him with burning phosphorous, and left him severely wounded. Flaming fragments within the helicopter caused supplies and ammunition to detonate. Dense white smoke filled the aircraft, obscuring the pilot's vision and causing him to lose control. Although having the use of only one arm and being partially blinded by the initial explosion, Sergeant Yano's indomitable courage and profound concern for his comrades averted loss of life and additional injury to the rest of the crew. By his conspicuous gallantry at the cost of his own life, in the highest traditions of the military service, Sergeant Yano has reflected great credit on himself, his unit and the United States Army."

Daniel J. Mulcahey, Brooks
Served in Vietnam, retired after 30 years

I am honoring Raymond Bechard, originally from Augusta, who was KIA in Vietnam in 1969. Ray and I were classmates as children.

Gary P. Burns, Augusta
Served in Vietnam

Raymond Bechard

I am voting in honor of my brother, Paul Joseph Frink. Paul was a Sergeant in the Army, Company D, 1st Battalion, 506th Infantry. He died in Vietnam on April 7, 1970, 5 days after his 21st birthday. He was awarded 11 separate military decorations and awards posthumously: Silver Star, Bronze Star, Air Medal, Army Commendation, Purple Heart, Good Conduct, National Defense Medal, Vietnam Campaign & Service Medals, Combat Infantryman's Badge and Sharpshooter's Badge. He is my hero.

According to newspaper accounts provided by his sisters, Sergeant Frink entered the service in February of 1969 and was sent to Vietnam in July of that year. He had distinguished himself by serving as a radio telephone operator during reconnaissance in "force operation" near fire support base Granite in the Republic of Vietnam.

While set up in a night defensive position, Sgt. Frink's unit came under an enemy sapper* attack.

Sgt. Frink was severely wounded, when a satchel charge exploded in his fighting position. Fearful that a call for help might direct the sapper force to other friendly positions, Sgt. Frink maintained silence despite the pain induced by his wounds.

With great courage he crawled under fire from his fighting position to his radio and called for friendly artillery and illumination. Sgt. Frink remained at his radio adjusting artillery fire until his physical condition made it imperative that he be evacuated.

Barbara Musmon, Saint Albans

*A sapper is a military engineer who specializes in field fortification activities, such as laying, detecting or disarming mines.

I am voting in honor of 2 buddies. Percy Gagnon was killed in action March 23, 1970, in 'Nam. He was a college classmate, teaching colleague, and fellow soldier. Stuart Woodman was killed in action June 6, 1970. I have dedicated each day of my life to their ultimate sacrifice.

Melford J. Pelletier, Wallagrass
Served in Vietnam, 1969-71

The following Maine voters used this opportunity to remember veterans whose names were on the MIA/POW bracelets they wore:

Roosevelt Hestle is an MIA from the Vietnam War. I wore an MIA bracelet of his for years. Last year my son placed it at the Vietnam Memorial in Washington, D.C. I never knew him, but I honor his sacrifice.

Joan Leavitt, Palmyra

Designed by Yale student Maya Ying Lin, the Vietnam Veterans Memorial was built to honor the memory of those who served in the Vietnam War. Over 58,000 names are etched in the black granite Memorial whose walls point towards the Washington Monument and Lincoln Memorial.

The person I am honoring, James Klimo, Specialist 5, is still MIA in Vietnam. I believe he was in the Army. His is the name on a POW/MIA bracelet that belonged to my mother.

Jennifer E.S. Ballweg, Waterville
Served during the Gulf War

Others respectfully remembered POW's or MIA's:

Howard David Stephenson and I grew up together on a farm, an apple orchard. He was MIA, shot down over Laos. His name is on the Wall in D.C. We're still waiting for him to come home.

Bruce W. Baker, Alexander
Served in Vietnam

I am voting in honor of Col. Donald G. Cook, USMC. He and I were POW's together in Vietnam, 1964-67.

According to an article enclosed by Mr. Crafts, *"In December 1964, Cook was ordered to the Communications Company, Headquarters Battalion, 3rd Marine Division in Saigon, Republic of Vietnam. On December 31, 1964, Cook volunteered to conduct a search and recovery mission for a downed American helicopter and set off with the 4th Vietnamese Marines. Ambushed on their arrival at the site, Donald was wounded in the leg and captured while attempting to rally his Vietnamese allies.*

Donald G. Cook

Cook was incarcerated in a prison camp near the Cambodian border and committed himself to providing inspiration for his fellow prisoners to endure and survive. He often surrendered his own rations and medicine to aid prisoners whose condition was more desperate than his own.

It was reported that he died in captivity from malaria on December 8, 1967. He was awarded the Medal of Honor in May, 1980, and the Aegis Destroyer DDG-75 built and launched in Bath, Maine, was named in his honor."

Charles Crafts, Livermore
Served in Vietnam

Edward Darcy is a POW/MIA from the Vietnam War. He has been missing since 1969.

Edith Dearborn, Mattawamkeag

I will be voting in honor of John Huntley, who was a POW and is still missing.

William B. Boone, Eastport

When I vote, I will do so in memory of the 15 Maine men listed as POW-MIA from Southeast Asia.

William A. Thomas, Lisbon Falls
Served in USAF in Vietnam

REMEMBER ME?

Home, America, the land I long to see
To you, a Symbol of the free,
Do you Remember me?

It's been so long since I've seen home
I'm oh so far away...
Can't anyone hear me...please listen to me say.

Memories now are all I have to help me through each day
Yet in my heart, a spark of hope
I know you'll find a way.

Please bring me home, my journey's end
I know how hard it's been
But Please you must keep trying,
This battle YOU must win.
I did my part, I fought my best
So others could be free
My destiny lies in YOUR hands
Please Remember Me.

Signed,
Away, but never alone
Never forgotten
As Long as I have all of you.

A POW-MIA

*Written by **Carole D. Thomas** in 1978*

---

*Responses like the following proudly pay tribute to **husbands** who served selflessly in Vietnam:*

I am voting in honor of my husband, Michael R. Brochu, Sr., who was a parachute rigger in the Navy. He volunteered for Vietnam and he would go again.

Nadine Brochu, Denmark

Michael R. Brochu, Sr.

My husband, J. Michel Patry, Sr., had a military career from 1965-1989. He served in Vietnam where he became disabled. Today he is an activist, a writer, a photographer, an educator, and an artist.

Evie Danika Patry, Lewiston

My husband, USAF Capt. Peter B. Smyth, served in the Vietnam Conflict. He was a dual-rated navigator/pilot whose mission was to refuel the fighters in mid-air. It is time that these Vietnam veterans are honored. These men served and sacrificed, some with their lives.

Evelyn Smyth, Rockland

I am voting in honor of my husband, Harry Gotham, who fought proudly and well for the freedom of other people in Vietnam from 1969-70.

Laurie Gotham, Buckfield

Harry Gotham

My husband, Everett A. Kaherl, served in the Air Force for 4 years during the Vietnam conflict and loaded bombs on planes. He became a law enforcement officer when he left the military and has been in law enforcement since then. He has 5 children and 9 grandchildren. He is a true and honest patriot.

Connie Kaherl, Lisbon

Everett A. Kaherl

My husband, Winfield "Jay" Sanborn, served in Vietnam as a paratrooper in the 101st Airborne. He has two Purple Hearts and I am very proud to be his wife.

Brenda Sanborn, Springvale

Winfield "Jay" Sanborn

Vietnam Women's Memorial

On Veterans Day in 1993, a bronze statue of three women and a wounded soldier was dedicated on the Mall in Washington, D.C. This statue, in close proximity to the Vietnam Wall, was placed in honor of the 265,000 women who served during the Vietnam era. It was a historic moment in time, for it was the first time a country has bestowed national recognition upon women who answered their country's call.

Other responses warmly praised the contributions of **women military personnel** *during this conflict:*

My wife, Melinda T. Goldberg, served 13 years in the U.S. Army Nurse Corps, including 2 tours in Vietnam. She attained the rank of Major.

Colonel Stuart E. Goldberg (Ret.), Portland
Served in Vietnam, 1971-72

I am voting in honor of my sister, Capt. Roberta MacLean, who was an Army nurse. She served in the field in the 7th Surgical Hospital Unit.

Ralph A. Mac Lean, South Portland
Served on USS Independence, Vietnam, 1965

Roberta MacLean

Sgt. Susanne Clark, LPN, was an Army nurse who served in Vietnam from December 1972 - February 1978. She is presently a staff nurse at the Greenwood Nursing Home in Sanford, where she is a wonderful nurse and co-worker.

James A. Walke, Springvale
Served as US Army Medic, 1979-89

Susanne Clark

1973 - 1975 – Peace talks resume in Paris on January 23, 1973. South Vietnamese communist forces, North Vietnam, South Vietnam, and the United States agree to a cease-fire. All U.S. Forces are to be withdrawn and all bases dismantled. The 17th parallel will remain the dividing line until the country can be reunited by "peaceful means."

But the fighting continues. Casualties are as high as they have ever been. In 1974 the North Vietnamese begin preparing for a major offensive while South Vietnam tries to hold the areas under its control. The North Vietnamese capture Phuoc Binh 60 miles north of Saigon in January 1975 and then begin a large-scale offensive in the central highlands in early March. The South Vietnamese military machine starts to unravel.

April 30, 1975 – The South Vietnamese government surrenders unconditionally. North Vietnamese tanks occupy Saigon. The last Americans leave Saigon, including 10 Marines from the United States Embassy.

July 2, 1976 – A military government is instituted and the country is officially united as the Socialist Republic of Vietnam with its capital in Hanoi.

Veterans with connections to Maine served during these final years of the war:

I will be voting in honor of my son, a brother, and 2 brothers-in-law. My brother, Peter Potter, served on a carrier in Vietnam, and my 2 brothers-in-law, Bill and Herb Larck, each served 3 tours in the Navy in Vietnam. My son, Leslie B. Potter, served 6 years in the Army; he died April 17, 1988.

Tice L. Potter, Kittery Point
Served in the Navy in WWII

More than 47,000 Americans were killed in action. Nearly 11,000 died of other causes. More than 303,000 were wounded in the war.

I will be voting in honor of the 343 Maine boys that died in Vietnam.

Linwood E. Green, Orono

"Linwood Green created Mobile Memories to preserve the history of the Vietnam War as it affected Maine families, and to encourage veterans of the controversial war to come out with dignity. The traveling exhibit memorializes the 343 Maine boys that were lost in Vietnam between 1964 and 1975 and highlights the history of Maine's involvement with photos, letters, and memorabilia of our Maine Vietnam Veterans."

Canadian Henry L. Dew was hoping to become an American citizen by joining the U.S. Army. According to a local newspaper story, PFC Dew had enlisted in the U.S. Army in Jackman in January of 1965 and was sent to Vietnam in October. He was killed by sniper fire at the age of 21. He is much loved and often remembered. It was an honor to have served with him.

Lester "Randy" Thompson, Houlton
Served during Vietnam, 1965-66

Henry L. Dew

I am voting in honor of Lt. Comdr. John McConnell. Flying a Crusader jet from the *USS Saratoga*, he spared my life and the lives of 150 others by staying with his out-of-control jet headed for us on deck. He could have ejected but didn't. It cost him his life, leaving behind his wife and family. I am now 60 years old, and I will never forget what this man did. He was a true hero. I wish I could tell his wife and kids what a great man their loved one was.

Charles Rideout, Bangor
Served during Vietnam era

I am voting in honor of my cousin, Capt. John "Jack" E. Duffy, a USAF Academy graduate. Jack was shot down over Vietnam while flying an observation aircraft. His body was returned to Maine only a few years ago, long after the deaths of his father, mother, and one brother.

Col. Richard D. Duffy, Belgrade
Serving in the Maine Army National Guard

Dana Gerald was a grade school and high school buddy who was killed in Vietnam.

Frederick W. Naborowsky, Vassalboro
Served in Vietnam, USAF (Ret.)

I am voting in honor of Bob Hauser. He was the first friend of mine that died in Nam.

Ray Weatherby, Rockland
Served in Vietnam

I am voting in honor of my neighbor, Leon Poland Jr. He and I were together for the last time in California when both of us were heading overseas.

Charles A. Lowe, Bryant Pond
Served in Vietnam, 1968-69

Leon Poland, Jr.

My half-brother, PFC Leon L. Poland, Jr., was a Marine from Woodstock, Maine, killed at Monkey Mountain near DaNang, Vietnam, on March 26, 1967. He was hit by a land mine while on patrol guarding an Air Force radar site.

Hazel R. Dillingham, South Paris

Leon Poland, Jr.

About 900,000 North Vietnamese and Viet Cong troops were killed. An unknown number were wounded. More than 1,000,000 North and South Vietnamese civilians were killed during the war.

The cost of the war is estimated at $200 billion.

I am honoring my brother-in-law, Ronald (Charles) Ouellette, who served in the Army during Vietnam. He returned home a doomed man with serious flashbacks. He passed April 26, 2000. He was 48.

Joseph A. Desrochers, Lewiston
Served in Vietnam

I am voting in honor of Larry Don Knippel. We went to NCO school together, roomed together at Ft. Hood, and I spent 3 days at his house before going to Vietnam together. He was killed on 3-13-70, but I didn't find that out until the last day of my first tour.

Charles M. Torno, Lebanon
Served in Vietnam, 1969-71

I am a 40% disabled service-connected veteran. Thank you for this program to honor veterans.

Russel S. Herbert, Portland
Served in Vietnam

I am voting in honor of my brother, Michael Gourley, a Marine who served in Vietnam. He was wounded 3 times, once in the head, and received the Purple Heart and medals for sharpshooting. He came home, but in a few years he committed suicide. He fought for his country as hard as he could.

Charlotte Stewart, Wellington

Michael Gourley

Evident throughout the responses about Vietnam veterans are compelling and unforgettable examples of heroism, dedication, and honor:

I am voting in honor of my brother, Edwin S. Dana, Sr. He served in the military for 28 years, including 3 tours in Vietnam in order, as he says, "to help my country and the buddies that I left behind."

Geneva Moulton, Bar Mills

My brother, Greg Tuholski, was drafted into the Army and killed in Vietnam.

Gerry Tuholski, Holden

My husband, Gerry Tuholski, joined the Air Force immediately after his brother Greg was killed in Vietnam.

Susan Tuholski, Holden

Thank you from all of us with hearts for the hurting. When we vote, we will be voting in honor of all hospitalized veterans and all homeless veterans. We give them value by remembering.

Lois Merrill, Kennebunk
Willis Merrill, Kennebunk
Served in Vietnam

Three Maine Medal of Honor Recipients from Vietnam Conflict

Sergeant Brian L. Buker, of Benton, served in the U.S. Army, Detachment B-55 5th Special Forces Group, 1st Special Forces. He received the Medal of Honor posthumously for "conspicuous gallantry and intrepidity in action at the risk of life above and beyond the call of duty," at Chau Doc Province, Republic of Vietnam, 5 April 1970. "Sergeant Buker distinguished himself while serving as platoon adviser of a Vietnamese mobile strike force company during an offensive mission. Sergeant Buker personally led the platoon, cleared a strategically located and well guarded pass, and established the first foothold at the top of what had been an impenetrable mountain fortress...As a direct result of his heroic actions, many casualties were averted, and the assault of the enemy position was successful. Sergeant Buker's extraordinary heroism at the cost of his life are in the highest traditions of the military service and reflect great credit upon him, his unit, and the U.S. Army."

Specialist Fourth Class Thomas J. McMahon, who entered the military in Portland, served in the U.S. Army, Company A, 2nd Battalion, 1st Infantry, 196th Brigade, American Division. He received the Medal of Honor posthumously by distinguishing himself while serving as medical aidman with Company A in Quang Tin Province, Republic of Vietnam on 19 March 1969. "When the lead elements of his company came under heavy fire from well fortified enemy positions, 3 soldiers fell seriously wounded. SP4 McMahon, with complete disregard for his safety, left his covered position and ran through intense enemy fire...He fell mortally wounded before he could rescue the last man. SP4 McMahon's undaunted concern for the welfare of his comrades at the cost of his life are in keeping with the highest traditions of the military service and reflect great credit on himself, his unit, and the U.S. Army."

Sergeant Donald S. Skidgel, of Caribou, served in the U.S. Army, Troop D, 1st Squadron, 9th Cavalry Division. He received the Medal of Honor posthumously for distinguished service as a reconnaissance section leader in Troop D near Song Be, Republic of Vietnam on 14 September 1969. "On a road near Song Be in Binh Long Province, Sergeant Skidgel and his section with other elements of his troop were acting as a convoy security and screening force when contact occurred with an estimated enemy battalion concealed in tall grass and in bunkers bordering the road...His selfless actions enabled the command group to withdraw to a better position without casualties and inspired the rest of his fellow soldiers to gain fire superiority and defeat the enemy. Sergeant Skidgel's gallantry at the cost of his life were in keeping with the highest traditions of the military service and reflect great credit upon himself, his unit, and the U.S. Army."

From **United States of America's Congressional Medal of Honor Recipients and Their Official Citations,** *provided by the Office of the Adjutant General, State of Maine*

International Incidents

Bay of Pigs Invasion (1961)

Tension between the United States and Cuba grew following the Cuban Revolution of 1959. Dictator Batista was ousted and revolutionary Fidel Castro came to power.

Prior to this revolution, the United States had had significant influence in the economy and politics of Cuba, but Castro did not want to be influenced by the U.S. Even when the United States applied economic pressure through an embargo that cut off trade, Castro refused to give in. In fact, he established even closer ties with the Communist government of the U.S.S.R.

In **January of 1961**, President Dwight D. Eisenhower had decided to break off formal diplomatic relations with Cuba. The Central Intelligence Agency had been training Cuban exiles for a possible invasion of the island as a means of overthrowing Castro's leftist regime without revealing U.S. involvement.

Most Cubans resented U.S. intervention in Cuban affairs, but Cuban exiles living in the United States worked with U.S. personnel to try to unseat Castro.

On **April 17, 1961,** approximately 1,300 United States-backed Cuban exiles, armed with U.S. weapons, unsuccessfully attempted to overthrow the government of Cuban Premier Fidel Castro in an invasion at the Bay of Pigs on the south coast of Cuba.

This brief military misadventure ended in total failure and quickly became a political and foreign policy debacle for President John F. Kennedy, who had approved the plan three months earlier.

The exiles had hoped to reach Havana, but, because they did not get support from the local people, Castro's army stopped them.

The fighting ended just 2 days later. About 100 of the Cuban exiles had been killed and the rest taken as prisoners. Despite information to the contrary from the Central Intelligence Agency, the Cuban people had never widely supported organized resistance to Castro's regime, so the plan may have been doomed from the start. Historians have called the Bay of Pigs "the perfect failure."

Forty years later, wariness and tension still characterize the relationship between the U.S. and Cuba, and Fidel Castro is still in power.

Fidel Castro

Maine military personnel who participated in activities associated with the **Bay of Pigs Invasion** *are remembered:*

I am voting in honor of my brother, Dennis A. Porter, who was born into a family of 7 sisters. He served on the *USS Hank* **that was stationed off Cuba during the Bay of Pigs Invasion. His home port was Norfolk, Virginia, and he served in the Navy for 4 years.**

Marlene J. Redlevske, Norridgewock

My brother, Gary Henry, served five years in the U.S. Navy as a Sonarman 2nd class and he was stationed in Vietnam and the Bay of Pigs in Cuba.

Robert Henry, Rockport
Served in the U.S. Navy

Cuban Missile Crisis (1962)

In 1962 there were growing concerns that the Soviet Union was preparing to secretly supply missiles to Cuba, missiles that could deliver nuclear warheads. This posed a particular risk to the U.S. with Cuba only 90 miles south of Florida.

"On October 14, 1962, U.S. spy planes flying over Cuba spotted the first ballistic missile. On October 16 U.S. intelligence officials presented Kennedy with photographs showing nuclear missile bases under construction in Cuba. The photos suggested preparations for two types of missiles: medium-range ballistic missiles able to travel about 1100 nautical miles and intermediate-range ballistic missiles able to reach targets at a distance of about 2200 nautical miles. These missiles placed most major U.S. cities – including Los Angeles, Chicago, and New York City – within range of nuclear attack. Kennedy also saw evidence of nuclear-capable bombers."

—from http://encarta.msn.com

The Kennedy administration faced a situation with potentially grave consequences. An attack on Cuba could trigger a global war, but ignoring the threat of this missile build-up could also risk war.

Kennedy and his advisors agreed that a surprise air attack against Cuba was the only reasonable response. However, some recommended a blockade as a possible prelude to negotiations. Kennedy went ahead with the blockade; at the same time, the U.S. military began moving soldiers and equipment into position.

In a worldwide radio and television address, Kennedy warned Khrushchev that if missiles were fired from Cuba, the response would be a "full retaliatory response upon the Soviet Union."

After a series of private negotiations and diplomatic maneuvers, on **October 28, 1962**, Khrushchev announced their decision to withdraw the missiles from Cuba in return for a "noninvasion pledge" from the United States.

A nuclear confrontation had been successfully avoided. The Cold War began to thaw as both super powers realized how close to the brink of nuclear war they had come.

John F. Kennedy
35th President of the United States

*Veterans who served in the military during the **Cuban Missile Crisis** were part of this dramatic chapter in world history:*

My brother-in-law, Archie L. Watt, Sr., was in the Army in the 60's during the trouble in Cuba.

Donna Chase, Dover Foxcroft

My father, Robert C. Leet, served in the U.S. Navy during the Cuban blockade in 1962.

Amy Leet, Millinocket

I served during the Cuban Crisis.

John E. McDonald, Jr., Mexico
U.S. Navy (Ret.)

We are voting in honor of our father, Boyd A. Young, who was in the Army during the Cuban Crisis in 1962.

Karen and James Young, Portland

We, too, are voting in honor of Boyd A. Young, father and father-in-law, who was drafted into the Army and was on a plane headed to Cuba during the Cuban Missile Crisis. At the last minute his plane was called back as the crisis had ended.

Lynn and Frank Kelley, Saco

My father, Ray Red, served in both Vietnam and during the Cuban Missile Crisis and is now retired from the U.S. Army.

Patricia D. Red, Topsham

*Wives wrote proudly about their **husbands'** service during the Cuban Missile Crisis:*

My husband, Don Cropley, served in the Army during the crisis in Cuba.

Valerie M. Cropley, East Millinocket

Don Cropley

I am voting in honor of my husband, Edward G. Tumosa, Jr., who served honorably in the U.S. Navy, including duty on the *USS Boston*, during the Cuban Missile Crisis. He was very proud to have served in the military for 4 years and said it was a great experience for him.

Joanne Tumosa, Newport

President John F. Kennedy and Chairman Nikita Khrushchev during their meeting in Vienna, Austria.

Berlin Wall (1969-1970)

At the end of World War II, the city of Berlin was partitioned into East and West Berlin. West Berlin was occupied by British, French, and United States forces and supported by the Federal Republic of Germany, usually known as West Germany. After this division, millions of people fled East Germany, many through Berlin, in order to have a higher standard of living.

Beginning in **August of 1961**, East Germany, identified as the German Democratic Republic (GDR), began to block off East Berlin from West Berlin with barbed wire and anti-tank obstacles. Tanks were stationed at crucial places, and subway lines and rail service between the two were interrupted. In the following days the temporary barriers were replaced by a solid wall.

The GDR called the wall protection from military aggression and political interference, but the western allies considered it a violation of Berliners' right to self-determination.

The Berlin Wall became a symbol of the Cold War tensions between the USSR and her communist allies and the western allies, led by the United States. The concrete wall was 12 feet high and 103 miles long. It cut through 192 streets, 97 leading to East Berlin and 92 into the GDR. Before its destruction, as many as 100 people may have been killed at the wall.

Veterans from Maine were stationed in Germany during this sometimes-tense Cold War standoff:

My brother, Craig F. Handley, served in the Army in Germany, 1969-1970.

Linda French, Smithfield

My identical twin brother, Spec 4 James E. Teves, was serving in the U.S. Army in Germany; while riding on a military vehicle, Jimmy came in contact with a high voltage line and died on July 7, 1975. I miss him.

John P. Huard (Teves), Albion
Served in Vietnam

James Teves

150

*Wives respectfully honor **husbands** who were stationed in Germany during this period:*

I am voting in honor of my husband, Roland F. Spellman, who served in the Army Infantry and patrolled the Fulda Gap section of the East German border during the Cold War.

Ruth-Marie Spellman, Brewer

Roland F. Spellman

My husband, Adrien Coulombe, served in the Army in Germany from 1964 to 1966.

Bernise Coulombe, Biddeford

I vote in honor of my husband, SSG Donald A. Gosselin, who served 11 years in the National Guard and 11 years in the Army Reserves, including duty during the Berlin Crisis.

Jeannine M. Gosselin, Lewiston

Donald Priest, my husband, served in the Army during the Berlin conflict, 1961-63.

Dianne Priest, North Anson

The Fall

During the **summer of 1989**, Hungary allowed East Germans to pass through Hungary on their way through to Austria and West Germany. By fall the East German regime had lost its power. On November 9, private citizens began to destroy entire sections of the concrete wall that had divided the city of Berlin for nearly 30 years. On November 22, new passages were opened north and south of the Brandenburg Gate, eliminating the separation that had divided the people of Germany since the end of World War II.

On **July 1, 1990**, an economic, monetary, and social union between East and West Germany is formed, and all travel restrictions are eliminated. The two Germany's are reunited as the Federal Republic of Germany.

Today a museum stands near the most famous crossing point, "Checkpoint Charlie," of what once was the infamous Berlin Wall.

Grenada (1983)

On **October 13, 1983**, the Grenadian army, controlled by former Deputy Prime Minister Bernard Coard, seized power in a bloody coup. The violence, coupled with the Marxist tendencies of the leadership, created concern among neighboring Caribbean nations as well as the United States. There was fear that the Cuban government was gaining influence in Grenada, and, even more pressing, nearly 1,000 American medical students were considered at risk.

The Reagan administration viewed this coup as part of a worldwide threat by the Soviet Union and other Communist countries, especially Cuba. The administration opted to confront this perceived expansion of Marxist influence in the Caribbean.

Early in the morning of **October 25, 1983**, the United States invaded Grenada in **Operation Urgent Fury**. Nearly 1,200 American troops met stiff resistance from the Grenadian army and Cuban military units on the island. When the invasion force grew to 7,000, the opposition fled or surrendered. By mid-December, a pro-American government was in control.

Maine military personnel were part of this conflict:

I am voting in honor of my wife, Isabel D. Raber, who has been serving for 30 years in the U.S. Army as a nurse. She served in Vietnam, Desert Storm and Grenada.

James M. Raber, Augusta
Served in Vietnam

Isabel D. Raber

I honor the service of my daughter, Jamie L. Mulcahey, who is in the Air Force and served in Lebanon and Grenada.

Daniel J. Mulcahey, Brooks
Served in Vietnam (Ret.)

Lebanon (1983)

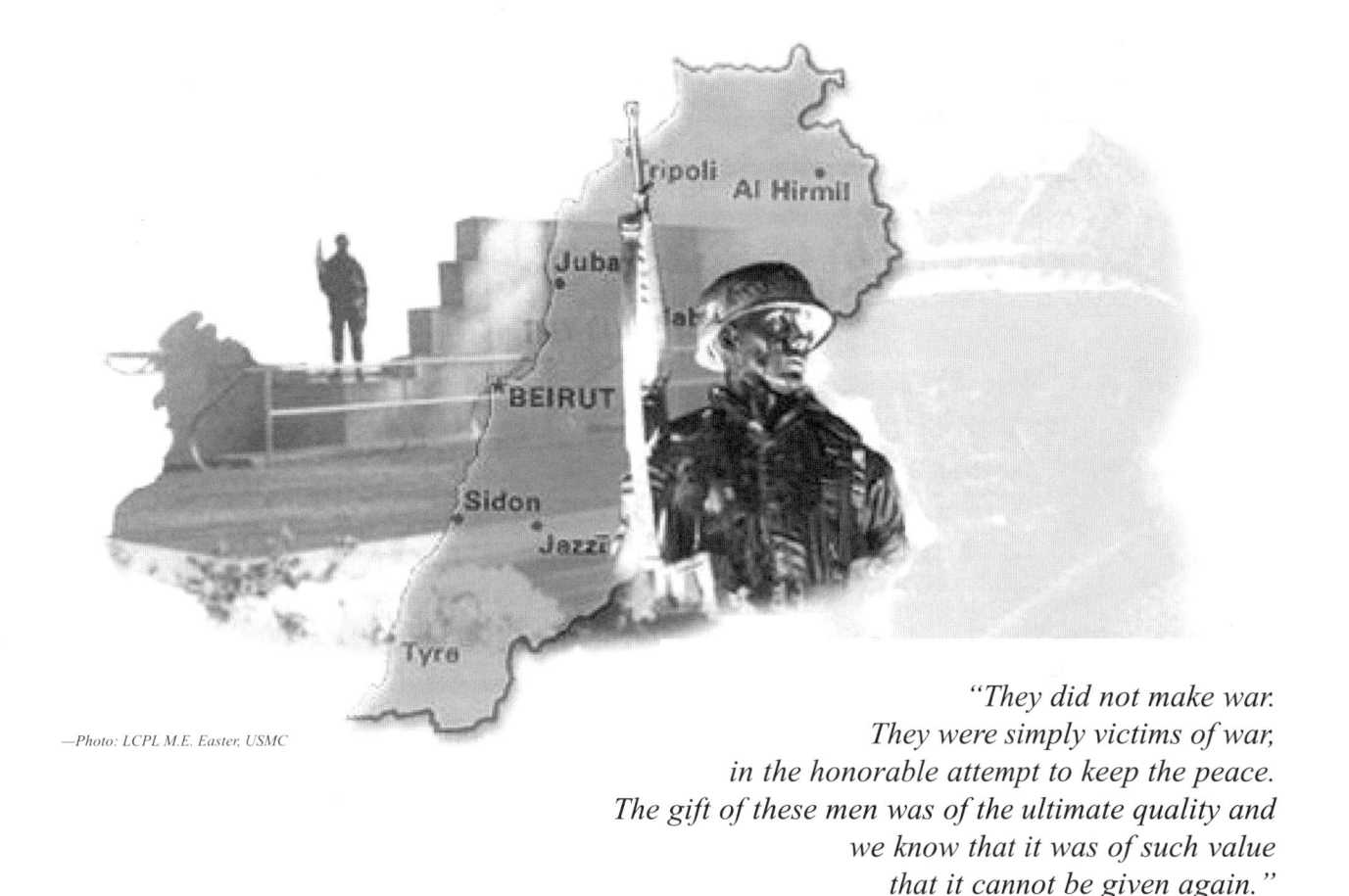

—Photo: LCPL M.E. Easter, USMC

> *"They did not make war.
> They were simply victims of war,
> in the honorable attempt to keep the peace.
> The gift of these men was of the ultimate quality and
> we know that it was of such value
> that it cannot be given again."*
>
> —from ***The Beirut Memorial Online***

On **April 18, 1983**, a terrorist, driving a van carrying a 2,000-pound load of explosives, tore through the front portion of the 7-story U.S. Embassy in Beirut, Lebanon.

The victims of this terrorist attack included 63 occupants of the building, 17 of whom were Americans. One Marine was killed, one journalist was killed, and the entire U.S. Central Intelligence Agency Middle East contingent were killed.

On **October 23, 1983**, a suicide bomber destroyed the Marine barracks in Beirut, killing 240 Marines.

I am voting in honor of my father, Roger A. Cobb, who served in the Marine Corps for over 26 years. He served 3 terms in Korea, went to Vietnam twice and was in <u>Beirut</u>. He lost his best friend when "the safest building" was blown up in Beirut!

Kimberly Hogan, Old Orchard Beach

I am voting in honor of Petty Officer Robert D. Stethem, a diver and underwater steelworker in the Seabees. I served with him in the Navy. He was the slain hostage aboard TWA flight #847 highjacked to Beirut, Lebanon on June 14th, 1985. He was returning from an assignment in Nea Makri, Greece when terrorists seized the aircraft. Petty Officer Stethem was singled out from the passengers and killed when terrorist demands were not met. He was posthumously awarded the Purple Heart and the Bronze Star. A Navy Aegis destroyer bears his name: *USS Stethem* (DDG 63).

Robert D. Stethem

Peter McKeown, Turner
Served in U.S. Navy, 1980-88

Reward Offered

"The Diplomatic Security Service of the U.S. Department of State offered a reward of up to $5,000,000 to bring the murderers of Navy Diver Robert Stethem to justice. The money is available under a program to obtain information that helps punish those responsible for past international terrorist acts against U.S. persons or property and prevent future such acts."

Panama (1989)

The invasion of Panama had as its key objectives the capture of Manuel Noriega and the establishment of a democratic government in Panama. In military action known as **Operation Just Cause**, America applied strong combat power when it was determined that it was no longer safe for U.S. military forces and other U.S. citizens in Panama.

On **December 20, 1989**, the 82nd Airborne Division conducted their first combat jump since WWII on to Torrijos International Airport, Panama.

The U.S. troops involved in **Operation Just Cause** achieved their primary objectives quickly, and troop withdrawal began on **December 27, 1989.**

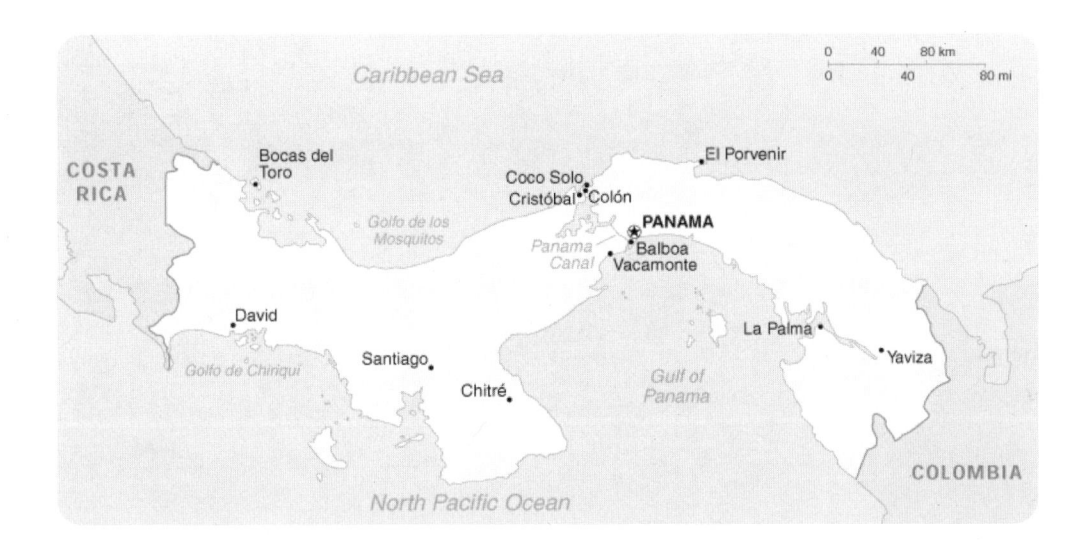

Maintaining Peace and Stability (1945-1990)

The Cold War years were a time of heightened tension around the globe. American troops were always "at the ready" in locations where peace was in jeopardy. Not only were U.S. forces sent to such places as Korea, Vietnam, and Lebanon when conflicts flared, but our troops also were stationed throughout the world to maintain stability and preserve peace.

Military service during this period included new challenges not previously experienced. Battle lines were less well drawn; in some cases, the enemy was less obvious. In many ways the stakes were higher because of sophisticated missile systems, advanced electronic and communication technologies, and, most obviously, the potential for nuclear war.

In their responses, Maine voters remember the service of veterans who defended the values of democracy, freedom, and independence during these unsettled decades of the Cold War:

When I vote, I will do so as a tribute to my husband, Maynard Warman, who served peacetime duty in the Navy from 1959 to 1963.

Wilma Warman, Belmont

I am voting in honor of my husband, David F. Kirkpatrick, a peacetime soldier stationed on the Mexican Border in El Paso, Texas. He was drafted during the Kennedy administration and served under President Lyndon Johnson.

Joan Kirkpatrick, Lincoln

I am voting in tribute to my husband, Mitchell B. Quint, who served in the USAF from 1954-57.

Emily Quint, North Anson

I am proud of my brother, Edward E. Hoyt III, who served in the USAF during the Cold War from 1977-79.

Theresa M. Hoyt, Fairfield

I am voting in honor of my son, L/Cpl Jason R. LeBarge, who served in the Marines for almost 4 years. His tour of duty ended when he was struck by a car and killed when he was returning to his base. He was 22 years old – he had never seen action – but he had traveled while a Marine and was prepared to defend his country.

Shirley B. LeBarge, Wells

Jason R. LeBarge

Jason's Footlocker

A footlocker, black, pockmarked with dents,
Kicked in at fun at a Cub Scout event,
Kanga Kangaroo, favorite Babar book
Fun Mad comics, first Playboy he took,
Worn camping gear, why the odd, old shoe?
Empty pig bank, rusty Matchbox cars crew,
Down near the bottom, locked tight they reside
Symbols of youth, in the trunk, side by side.
Boy Scout badges, coins and stamps,
Prom picture, blue tuxedo at his Senior dance
Yearbook '80, baseball cards and knotted twine,
Drama scripts, football jersey, number nine.
Leather mitt, "leftie," and bat,
Hunting vest and bright orange hat.
Proud photo, first deer, it was a stag
Our letters from home in a brown paper bag.
A final trophy, his last ever to be
Dear God, I, his mother, store here –
In his footlocker, black
In the attic way in back –
Along with a Marine Corps tag,
I sadly place (it's red, white and blue),
Jason's tri-folded, American flag.

by Shirley Boothby LeBarge

We are proud to vote in honor of Gerard Routhier, who served in the U.S. Marines and was stationed in Iceland in the early '60's.

Florida Routhier, Wife, Fairfield
William H. Routhier, Son, Fairfield
Ms. Beverly Routhier, Daughter, Waterville

I am voting in honor of my husband, Roland Scribner. He was a Corporal in the 278th Regimental Combat Team in the First Army stationed in Iceland, 1961-62.

Joan Scribner, Lee
Served during the Korean War era

I am proud of my husband, Norman C. Dickey. He served in the Air Force from 1957-1962 and was stationed at Wethersfield Air Force Base in England where we met and married in 1960. We moved to Skowhegan where we have resided ever since.

Patricia A. Dickey, Skowhegan

My husband, Arlan Dakin, was in the Army National Guard and was injured during his service in the 1970's. He is 100% disabled.

Sylvia Dakin, Belfast

I am voting in honor of my friend, Romeo J. Bouchard, who served in the Army in 1974-75.

Nora Heffelfinger, Woodland

From November, 1979 through July, 1984, I served in the USAF as a Medical Technician. Then I became a Weather Observer at Loring AFB until I separated from active duty in 1986.

Debra A. Parent, Limestone

We want to pay tribute to Tom Schneller, husband and father, for his service in the U.S. Navy as a sonar technician. He was on active duty from 1973-75 and in the Reserves from 1975-77. He assisted in evacuating U.S. civilians when Turkey invaded Cyprus.

Alison Schneller, Wife, Scarborough
Erika Schneller, Daughter, Scarborough

My daughter, Cecilia K. Bralick, served 4 years in the USAF in Turkey as a Language Specialist.

Bertrand M. Dyer, Sr., North New Portland
Served in Korea and Vietnam

I am voting in honor of my husband, Robert E. Molinaro. He was in uniform when I first met him and it was love at first sight…his penetrating and sincere eyes made me believe he was the one for me. He served on active duty from May, 1972-September, 1992, retiring as a Lieutenant Colonel, Military Police Corps, U.S. Army.

Marcene J. Molinaro, Kennebunkport

I honor all veterans, male and female, who came back from all wars, conflicts, and police actions, in pieces, both mental and physical, and especially those who were POW, KIA and MIA.

Charles E. Blackman, Boothbay Harbor
Served active duty 1957-1976, USN (Ret.)

I will be voting in honor of all veterans that have gone before me for the sacrifices they have made throughout their service to this country.

Stanley P. Follett, Westbrook
Served from 1961-1988

Chapter 4

THE WORLD'S PEACEKEEPERS

The Persian Gulf War (1990-1991)

"I have seen in your eyes a fire of determination to get this war done quickly. My confidence in you is total, our cause is just. Now you must be the thunder and lightning of Desert Storm."

General H. Norman Schwarzkopf
Commander in Chief, U.S. Central Command
Commander of Operations of Desert Shield
and Desert Storm
U.S. Army, Retired

—*U.S. Army photo*

A series of events lead up to the involvement of United Nations' troops in the Persian Gulf in order to ease conflicts over oil production and military build-up in the region.

July 15-17, 1990 – Iraq accuses Kuwait of stealing oil from the Rumaylah oil field on the Iraq-Kuwait border and warns of military action.

July 22, 1990 – Iraq begins its military buildup against Kuwait.

August 2, 1990 – Iraq invades Kuwait. The United Nations Security Council condemns Saddam Hussein for the Iraqi invasion and calls for the immediate and unconditional withdrawal of the Iraqi forces. President George Bush freezes Iraqi and Kuwaiti assets.

August 6, 1990 – Economic sanctions are authorized.

August 8, 1990 – Iraq annexes Kuwait.

August 9, 1990 – The Security Council imposes full economic and military sanctions against Iraq.

August 10, 1990 – Hussein declares a "jihad," or holy war, against the U.S. and Israel.

August 25, 1990 – The U.N. Security Council calls for the use of force, if necessary, to compel Iraq to withdraw from Kuwait.

September 14, 1990 – Iraqi forces storm a number of diplomatic missions in Kuwait City.

November 29, 1990 – The Security Council sets a deadline of January 15th for the peaceful withdrawal of Iraqi forces from Kuwait.

*Maine citizens pay tribute to **Desert Storm** peacekeepers:*

I am voting in honor of Lieutenant General Calvin Waller (deceased). LTG Waller was a soldier's soldier. He served in Vietnam and was General Norman Schwarzkopf's deputy command in <u>Desert Storm</u>.

Colonel J.T. Cuccaro, Freeport
Served 2 tours in Vietnam, U.S. Army (Ret.)

My husband, John Nelson, served 16 years active duty. He advanced from E-1 to Major and was awarded the Bronze Star for service as a medical officer in the <u>Persian Gulf War</u>. He is now in the National Guard and still serving as an Aviation Physician Assistant, U.S. Army.

Hattie Nelson, Lincoln
Served in the Women's Army Corp

I am honoring my spouse, Hans W. Heins, who gave twenty years of his life to keep all of us safe. Every day he served was one day each one of us had one more day of freedom. His belief was to serve his country with his heart and soul, to honor and obey, and to die for her if the need may come, and I am proud of him for this.

He joined the Navy in 1976, the end of the Vietnam War. But he still got over there to fix downed aircraft. He also served during <u>Desert Storm</u>. In the twenty years he served it was not done as a job; it was a choice, a choice he would do again.

I would also like to honor all the other veterans that served as well, the ones that never came home, and the ones that did. I honor all who served in all our wars, from the Minutemen to the most current soldiers. They did so from the desire to do something for their country and the people they loved, and now it's our time to honor them all.

Patricia E. Heins, West Gardiner

I am voting in honor of AK1 Debra L. Matchett, who served 20 years in the Navy and was an intricate part of <u>Desert Storm</u>.

Layne Curtis, Lisbon

Debra L. Matchett

I pay tribute to my aunt, Rhoda Sinatra, who served in Operation <u>Desert Storm</u> and is retired Navy.

Yussif Rishani, Bangor

My son, Chester W. Goggin, is retired from the U.S. Navy after 20 years of service, including duty in Vietnam and <u>Desert Storm</u>. Also, I honor my son Richard J. Goggin, who was killed in Vietnam, my daughter Donna E. Goggin, a 20-year Air Force veteran, and my brother Donald C. Eye, who was a 20-year Navy veteran.

Thelma E. Brooks, Waterville

I am voting in honor of my daughter, Pamela J. Farnsworth, PNC (Ret.), who served in the U.S. Navy from 1973 – 1996 during Vietnam and Desert Storm.

Virginia Farnsworth, Bar Harbor

Pamela J. Farnsworth

My niece, Debby (Elderkin) Willis, deserves to be honored when we vote. She was in the Army and was a hostage in Kuwait. Now she is a civilian and is a lawyer.

Patricia Johnson, Parkman

Debby Willis

January 15, 1991 – The deadline of the U.N. Resolution 678 for Iraq to withdraw expires at midnight.

January 16, 1991 – Allied forces begin **Operation Desert Storm** with a massive air offensive. U.S. warplanes attack Iraqi forces in Kuwait and military targets in Iraq.

January 17, 1991 – Iraq launches its first SCUD Missile attack.

February 1, 1991 – U.S. Secretary of Defense warns that the U.S. will retaliate if Iraq uses chemical or unconventional weapons.

February 8, 1991 – The total number of U.S. troops in the Gulf is now over a half million.

February 25, 1991 – Iraqi SCUD missile hits a U.S. barracks in Dhahran, Saudi Arabia, killing 27 U.S. soldiers.

February 27, 1991 – President Bush orders a cease-fire effective at midnight Kuwaiti time. President Bush declares Kuwait liberated.

March 3, 1991 – Iraqi leaders formally accept the cease-fire.

March 4, 1991 – First allied POWs freed.

March 5, 1991 – Remaining POWs released.

My son, LTJG. James B. (Jeb) Shields, was killed in the line of duty on March 21, 1991, when two P3 Orions collided in the sky off the coast of California.

Bethel B. Shields, Auburn

James B. Shields

April 3, 1991 – The U.N. Security Council approves the cease-fire agreement in the Gulf and calls on Iraq to respect the boundaries, pay war compensation and destroy chemical, biological, and nuclear weapons.

Gulf War Troops Return Home

Approximately 697,000 U.S. troops served during **Operation Desert Shield** and **Desert Storm**. When troop carriers first began returning home, crowds of Mainers greeted flights returning from the Persian Gulf at the Bangor International Airport to give U.S. soldiers an all-American welcome.

> **I am voting to honor my brother, Charles "Chuck" Nute. He was a medic serving with the 11th Arm. Cav. 37th Med Co in the late 60's. He met every <u>Desert Storm</u> flight coming into Bangor.**
>
> *Steve Nute, Belfast*
> *Served during the Vietnam era*

Television viewers across the country watched as Sgt. Kevin Tillman, among the first soldiers to receive the Bangor "welcome home" greetings, performed his impromptu rendition of "The Star-Spangled Banner" on a saxophone borrowed from a musician in the John Bapst Memorial High School band.

Sgt. Kevin Tillman plays "The Star Spangled Banner" at Bangor International Airport.
—*Bangor Daily News photo*

When the last official flight departed from Bangor on **May 27, 1991**, crowds in Maine's Queen City had enthusiastically welcomed home an estimated 100,000 Gulf War soldiers. To commemorate these acts of kindness, Everett Steele, himself a Korean veteran, helped organize a 10-year reunion on March 7, 2001, at Bangor International Airport, for those who had been part of the Bangor Homecoming festivities. Steele estimates that he and a handful of others had greeted 350 flights since that first carrier landed.

Sgt. Tillman, in remarks made during that anniversary reception, remembers the enthusiastic outpouring of patriotism and gratitude that greeted him on his return home:

"If the first troop carriers had not come to Maine, and not come to Bangor, what did happen may not have happened. By rising to the occasion...and setting the standard for the rest of the country and how we take care of our military personnel, you all left no doubt...why we do what we do."

—*from the **Bangor Daily News**, March 8, 2001*

Somalia (1992 – 1994)

December 1992 – A U.N. peacekeeping force, including 2,000 U.S. Marines, is sent to restore order between warring factions in Somalia. Other international agencies attempt to distribute food and other humanitarian aid. For the first time ever, the United Nations is engaged in an "armed humanitarian intervention" called **Operation Restore Hope**.

U.N. peacekeeping forces eventually become involved in the violence and a number of U.N. soldiers are killed. In **October 1993**, the U.S. ends its five-month search for General Aidid after 18 U.S. soldiers are killed and some of their corpses are dragged through the streets of Mogadishu. International pressure becomes more intense. In **1994** U.N. forces are withdrawn.

I am voting in honor of my brother-in-law, Staff Sergeant Thomas J. Field, who served on a Blackhawk helicopter in the Army. He had just recently re-enlisted and was engaged to be married when he was shot down in <u>Somalia</u>. His body was dragged through the streets as a trophy. He is truly missed.

Shannon R. Voigt, Lisbon Falls

Master Sergeant Gary L. Gordon, of Lincoln, while serving in the U.S. Army in Somalia, "distinguished himself by actions above and beyond the call of duty on 3 October 1993, as Sniper Team Leader, United States Army Special Operations Command with Task Force Ranger in Mogadishu, Somalia. Master Sergeant Gordon's sniper team provided precision fires from the lead helicopter during an assault and at two helicopter crash sites...He and another sniper unhesitatingly volunteered to be inserted to protect the four critically wounded personnel...Equipped with only his sniper rifle and a pistol, Master Sergeant Gordon and his fellow sniper...fought their way through a dense maze of shanties and shacks to reach the critically injured crew members...Then, armed only with his pistol, Master Sergeant Gordon continued to fight until he was fatally wounded. His actions saved the pilot's life. Master Sergeant Gordon's extraordinary heroism and devotion to duty were in keeping with the highest standards of military service and reflect great credit upon his unit and the United States Army."

*from **United States of America's Congressional Medal of Honor Recipients and Their Official Citation**, provided by the Office of the Adjutant General, State of Maine*

In **mid-1994**, the last of the U.S. troops leave Somalia. Somali leaders continue fighting. International relief organizations suspend their operations.

No military, political or economic solutions have yet been found to alleviate the unrest in Somalia.

Haiti (1994)

Throughout the 1990s the international community devotes considerable effort to establishing democracy in Haiti. The country's first elected chief executive, Jean-Betrand Aristide, a Roman Catholic priest, is sworn in as president on February 7, 1991. The military, however, takes control. A multinational peacekeeping force, led by the United States but under the auspices of the United Nations' **Operation Uphold Democracy**, arrives in **1994.** U.S. soldiers leave in 2000, but U.N. peacekeepers remain. With unemployment of at least 50%, Haiti has turned into a major drug shipment point between Colombia and the U.S. A steady flow of refugees has been arriving in the U.S., often in leaky boats. Despite the international emphasis on democracy, Haiti's government is paralyzed, and lacks the rudiments of a modern civil society, such as an independent court system, parliament, and administrative bureaucracy.

U.N. peacekeepers.

Kosovo (1999 – present)

After World War II Yugoslavia (formed in 1918 after the fall of the Austro-Hugarian Empire) becomes a communist republic under Prime Minister Tito. It is comprised of 6 republics – Serbia, Croatia, Bosnia-Herzegovina, Macedonia, Slovenia, and Montenegro – as well as 2 provinces, Kosovo and Vojvodina.

1980 – Ethnic tensions begin to flare after Tito's death.

1991 – Slovenia and Croatia each declare independence. Slovenia breaks away with only a minimum of fighting. However, because 12% of Croatia's population is Serbian, Yugoslavia fights hard against its secession for the next four years.

1992 – Bosnia-Herzegovina declares independence. Bosnia is the most ethnically diverse of the Yugoslav republics: 42% Muslim, 31% Serbian, and 17% Croatian. Tension is high and Bosnia erupts into war.

1995 – A fragile peace is achieved and the country is partitioned into three areas, each governed by one of the three ethnic groups

Serbia and Montenegro form the Federal Republic of Yugoslavia with Slobodan **Milosevic** as its leader. The U.S. does not recognize this new government as the successor to the former Yugoslavia.

1996 – In the southern province of Kosovo, militants begin attacking Serbian police.

1998 – **Milosevic** sends troops to the province of Kosovo to stop the unrest. Guerilla war breaks out.

1999 – Peace talks fail and the North Atlantic Treaty Organization (NATO) threatens to launch airstrikes on Serbian targets. NATO intervenes in Kosovo in **Operation Allied Force** on March 26, and action continues until June 10. NATO-led international peace-enforcement forces attempt to restore stability in what was determined to be a strategic region lying between Alliance member states. According to NATO records, more than 38,000 sorties were flown, without a single Allied fatality.

Security forces (KFOR) totaling over 46,000 military personnel from 39 countries are deployed on **June 12** in **Operation Joint Guardian**, a multinational effort with substantial NATO participation.

NATO forces have been at the forefront of humanitarian efforts in this region. Of particular concern has been the treatment of Albanian refugees and other abuses of human rights during this period of "ethnic cleansing" perpetrated by the Milosevic-led forces.

It has been estimated that by the end of **May 1999**, 1.5 million people have been expelled from their homes in Kosovo. At least 5,000 Kosovars have been executed, and 225,000 Kosovar men are believed to be missing.

New elections are held in **2000**, but Milosevic refuses to release the complete results. Citizens are outraged. A general strike is called. Mobs attack the Parliament building and Milosevic's support diminishes. Milosevic steps down. The United States and the European Union begin to lift economic sanctions, but peacekeeping troops remain in the region.

Given this history, building peace in Kosovo will continue to be a long-term commitment on the part of the international community.

—USAID photo

I am voting in honor of my son, Robert M. P. Roy, who is in the U.S. Navy. He was stationed first on the *USS Theodore Roosevelt* and now is on the *USS Harry S. Truman*. He was only 18 years old when he went to the war in <u>Kosovo</u>. He was scared but honored to represent the United States of America. He was ready to give up his life.

Janey Rivard, Lisbon

Robert M. P. Roy

Chapter 5

LIFETIMES OF SERVICE: CAREERS AND FAMILIES

Career Military

No collection of tributes honoring Maine veterans would be complete without a special section dedicated to those military personnel who made military service their careers. Their dedication, service, and commitment to their country distinguish their professional lives in ways that deserve special recognition.

Among the thousands of requests received by the Secretary of State's office to **Vote in Honor of a Veteran**, scores of them were tributes to veterans who had military careers spanning decades and including duty in several major military engagements. Some even served in more than one branch of the military.

*The following samples represent responses that proudly honor **husbands** who made the military their careers:*

> **I am voting in honor of my husband, Robert W. Field, who served in WWII, Korea, and Vietnam. His active duty was in the U.S. Navy from 1945-1971, when he retired as a Master Chief.**
>
> *Maxine L. Field, Ellsworth*

> **My husband, Kevin Fortin, served in the Army for 22 years. He went to Korea and then Vietnam early in that war and did real well serving his country. He accomplished a lot on behalf of our family.**
>
> *Evelyn Fortin, Van Buren*

> **I will be proud to vote in honor of my husband, Albert Friedman, AFCM Navy Retired, who served his country with pride. His love of the Navy was an example to all who served with him. We have been married for 53 years, but he has been in a nursing home since last April; his thoughts of his years in the Navy are all his own now.**
>
> *Mrs. Hyla Friedman, Jay*

Albert Friedman

I am voting in honor of my husband, Daniel Gatchell, who served 3 years in the U.S. Army, one of them in Vietnam. Then he served 21 years in the U.S. Coast Guard; he was stationed on icebreakers and participated in search and rescue missions and drug enforcement activities, and spent 12 months on isolated duty on the island of Iwo Jima. He retired in 1993 as a Warrant Officer.

Judythe Gatchell, Brunswick

I pay tribute to my husband, Raymond E. Bland, who entered the Marine Corps in 1948. He served in Korea and received the Purple Heart; he also served in Vietnam and retired in 1974. He is very proud of his service to his country and proud of the USMC.

Ruth L. Bland, Wells

Raymond E. Bland

My husband, Richard F. Alexander, Sr., served 21 years in the U.S. Coast Guard. He was in the first Tet Offensive in Vietnam in 1967-68 aboard a CG cutter serving with coastal surveillance forces.

Joyce Alexander, South Portland

I will proudly vote in honor of my husband, Fred J. Bowers, Jr., who retired from the Army Air Corps after 30 years of service and is now deceased. He was a radioman during WWII, was wounded, and received the Purple Heart.

Lois H. Bowers, Bangor

Fred J. Bowers, Jr.

I am paying tribute to my husband, Sidney T. Lewis, retired Colonel and physician in the USAF. He served in Vietnam, was a Clinic Commander in the Canal Zone and at Hanscam AFB in Massachusetts, Director of Professional Services at WPAFB in Ohio, and teacher at Brooks AFB in Texas.

Hilda M. Lewis, Eastport
Served in Operation Desert Storm

*Sons and daughters voted in honor of **fathers** whose examples of patriotism and dedication to duty inspired them:*

I am voting in honor of my father, Gerald Murphy, who served from 1947-67 and retired as a U.S. Navy Chief. He did 3 tours in Vietnam on the *Ranger*, the *Constellation*, and the *Midway*. My father taught us patriotism by living it. He was very proud to be in the Navy and taught all 3 of his children to be proud to be U.S. citizens.

Diane Whispell, Durham

Our father and father-in-law, Simon L. Soctomah, is a full-blooded Passamaquoddy, who served in the Infantry in WWII and also the Korean War, during which he was wounded. He is the father of 7 children and was proud to have served his country.

Lena Jackson, Londonderry, NH , daughter
Kenneth Jackson, son-in-law
Served in Vietnam

I am proud to vote in honor of both of my parents, Earl and Mary Doliber. My father served in the Navy in WWII and then in the Army with service in Korea and Vietnam until 1966. My mother faithfully followed him from posting to posting, including trips overseas 3 times, and she raised 5 children on the way.

Dana E. Doliber, Sanford
Served in Vietnam, 1967-68

We are proud to be voting in honor of our parents, John and Hattie Nelson. Both served in the U.S. Army. Dad was a hero in the Gulf War and served 16 years active duty. Mom "wore combat boots" in the Women's Army Corps.

Nick and Jennifer Nelson, Lincoln

I am proud of my father, William Harold Knobel, who served in the USMC from 1942–1970, with duty in WWII, the China occupation, Korean peacekeeping efforts (1953) and Vietnam (1965-66).

David Knobel, J.D., Sabattus

I am voting in honor of my father, James Watts, who served in both WWII and Vietnam. He influenced me to join the Navy and to serve my country proudly.

Diane Turcotte, Skowhegan
Served in Vietnam

I am proud of my dad, John L. Ketner, Sr., who served in the Navy for 30 years. He served on the *USS Pittsburg* in WWII and the *USS Houston* in the China seas and did several tours in the Pacific. I am very proud of him.

John L. Ketner, Jr., Farmingdale
Served in the Korea, "forgotten war"

My father, William P. Curran, served in the Army for 22 years. His duty included Pearl Harbor, Guadalcanal, the Solomon Islands, Luzon, Philippines, New Caledonia and Korea. During his service he won the Silver Star with Oak Leaf cluster and the Purple Heart.

Bernadette A. Curran Steele, Waldoboro

John C. Hanusek, Sr.
(1944)

I would like to honor my father, John C. Hanusek, Sr., because he has told me many interesting and sad stories of the days he faithfully served. I feel all people should duly respect all veterans for what they did for us. Not enough can be said and done to honor our veterans. I honor my daddy, the flag, and am very proud to say my father has honored and served our country. He taught me the value of life and laughter. With great respect he served on the *USS Fargo* in the Navy in WWII and as an airplane machinist in the USAF during the Korean Conflict.

John C. Hanusek, Sr.
(1952)

Tina Antoine, Saco

Other Maine citizens pay tribute to a family member's lifetime of public service:

We are voting in honor of <u>our grandfather</u>, CWO4 Robert J. Gillis Jr., who served for 26 years in the USAF, with duty during WWII, the Korean Conflict, and Vietnam. He retired to Calais, where he remained active in local politics and served as mayor, state representative, and county commissioner.

Rod E. Tirrell, Calais
Theresa Milton, Calais

I am voting in honor of <u>my wife</u>, Charlotte C. Robertson, who served in the Navy Medical Corps during WWII and Korea.

William P. Robertson III, Franklin
Served in WWII and Korea

Charlotte C. Robertson

I am voting in honor of <u>my brother</u>, George F. Lovejoy, who served in the Navy, in WWII and the Korean Conflict. He served as Acting Chief, Aviation Machinist Mate on the aircraft carrier *Valley Forge* and was decorated twice for saving aviators from planes on fire on the deck of the carrier.

<u>My father</u>, George F. Lovejoy, Sr., joined the Navy in 1918 when he was only 15 years old to serve in WWI. Then he served in the Massachusetts National Guard from 1930 until 1940. In 1941, with the threat of war on the horizon, his unit was activated and federalized. He served in the Pacific Theater for the duration of the war. Lt. Col. Lovejoy was awarded the Bronze Star and a number of other citations for action in the Pacific.

George F. Lovejoy, Jr.

George F. Lovejoy, Sr.

His division was pinned down by a superior enemy force for an entire month. We only learned of our father's safety when neighbors of ours in Saugus (Massachusetts) told us that they had seen his picture in a February, 1943 issue of <u>Life</u>. We confirmed that it was indeed his picture and he later acknowledged that he had been photographed overlooking Henderson Field after its recapture by the Americans.

James E. Lovejoy, Unity

Pride in veterans' military careers continues:

We are voting in honor of <u>our uncle</u>, Peter P. Lenosky, who joined the Army Air Force right out of high school. He served in the USAF from 1945-1965. He served his country all over the world and then returned home to raise six children. He loved Maine and Loring AFB. He remained fiercely patriotic until his death 2 years ago.

Carole Reid, Scarborough
Richard W. Reid, Scarborough

I am voting in honor of Edward Hoyt II, who served in the Air Force during the Korean War and the Marines during the Vietnam War. He has been very active in veterans' groups and veterans' activities.

Jeanne C. Kempers, Fairfield

Edward Hoyt II

<u>My brother</u>, Ron Bennett, retired as an E-7 after serving 20 years with the Navy Seabees in Cuba, Antarctica, and Vietnam.

Paul L. Bennett, Lebanon

From 1952-1976 I proudly served in the U.S. Air Force with duty in both Korea and Vietnam.

Horatio S. Couture, Benton

I am one of a few in Maine that served in 3 conflicts.

Chauncey Gerry, North Waterboro
Served in WWII, Korea, and Vietnam

I served in the U.S. Coast Guard for more than 20 years. My back was nearly broken in a fall during a search and rescue operation in the North Atlantic. There was a hurricane and the wind was 50 mph and the waves were 40 feet high.

Felix Y. Atienza, Jr., Windham
Served during Vietnam era

The Sacrifices of Families

Compelling responses describe the dedication, commitment and service of entire **families**. The following accounts remind us of the sacrifice and honor associated with military service…and the debt we all owe these gallant and unselfish servicemen and women and the families who love them.

*Many Maine voters honored **brothers** who represented their families in military service:*

> **I am voting in honor of <u>my 5 brothers</u>: Frank, Joseph, William, George and Edward Vrba. Frank served as a Medic in Italy, Joseph in the Army Air Force in Burma, William in the Infantry in Newfoundland, and George in the Infantry in Iran. Edward served in the Infantry and was killed during the Battle of the Bulge – he was just 21 years old. Our mother, Barbara Vrba, was a <u>Gold Star Mother</u> of 6 honored WWII veterans.**

Jerry Vrba, Brewer
Served in the Philippines, Korea, and stateside

GOLD STAR MOTHERS

The term "**Gold Star Mothers**" applies to mothers whose sons or daughters died while in service to our country. The Gold Star symbolizes the honor and glory accorded a person for supreme sacrifice for his or her country and the devotion and pride of the family in this loved one's sacrifice. American Gold Star Mothers, Inc. was founded nationally after the First World War to "perpetuate the ideals of Americanism for which their children had so gallantly fought and died."

For more information see www.goldstarmoms.com.

> **I am voting in honor of <u>my 3 brothers</u>, Loring, Gardner, and Lorenzo Creamer. Loring served in the U.S. Army at home, Gardner in the U.S. Navy in the Pacific, and Lorenzo in the U.S. Air Force in Europe.**

Mrs. Frances Creamer Richardson, Friendship

Gardner L. Creamer

Lorenzo C. Creamer

I am paying tribute to my 3 brothers, Robert, James, and Steven, all of whom enlisted in the military during the Vietnam conflict. It was a time of honoring their country.

My oldest brother Robert joined the Navy and was sent to Subic Bay, Philippines, where he was a Navy photographer and flew frequent missions over Vietnam. My brother James also joined the Navy and became a boilerman on a submarine. My youngest brother, Steven, struggled to follow his brothers into military service. He was below weight requirements and made several trips to Des Moines for his physical before finally being accepted. He served in the Air Force in Thailand and then stateside.

I also honor my nephew, Dan Grant, who joined the Air Force and was stationed at Clark Air Base in the Philippines. My husband, brother, and nephew often met in the Philippines – they were family a half a world away from home, a small town in Iowa.

Following in his father's footsteps, my husband, James Mathis, enlisted in the Navy. He was sent to Vietnam and was stationed aboard the *USS Sanctuary*. He served as a corpsman in the operating room where he saw the worst cases of men who would be "patched up," many with amputations, and then taken by medivac to the Philippines and elsewhere for further medical care. It was very traumatic for a young man from a small town, and it still affects him to this day.

This war had a great impact on all of our family. It seems we were always seeing one of them off or welcoming one home. Thankfully, my husband, my 3 brothers and my nephew, young men all, returned to us.

I am very proud of each one of them and grateful that they chose to serve their country during a time when it was not a popular thing to do. I have great respect for all who serve and I am grateful for the duty they feel.

Royann Mathis, West Bowdoin

The Gilbert Boys
Top Row: Armand, Richard and Joseph
Bottom Row: Lionel, Gerald and Alfred

I am voting in honor of the 6 Gilbert brothers, all of whom served honorably: Armand, Lionel, Alfred, Joseph, Richard, and Gerald. Armand served in the South Pacific, Lionel in Normandy, Omaha Beach, France and Germany, Alfred in the USAF in France, Germany and Okinawa, Joe in the USMC in Germany, Richard in the USMC, and Gerald in the US Army in Korea. I am the only one left.

Joseph O. Gilbert, Augusta
Served in WWII and Korea

I want to honor my 6 brothers. Emile, Julien, and Dollard served in the European Theater; Laurier and Ivan served in the Marines; Real was in the Naval Seabees in the Pacific Theater.

Richard J. Dupont, Jay

I will be voting in honor of the 4 Levesque brothers: Omer served in France during WWII; Camille served during WWII in Luzon and the Philippines; Conrad served in the Air Force in the 60's, and I was a Marine in Korea.

Josephat N. Levesque, West Paris
Served in the Marines in Korea, 1953-55

Upper Left: Josephat Levesque
Upper Right: Conrad Levesque
Lower Left: Camille Levesque
Lower Right: Omer Levesque

I am proud of the military service of all of us Adams brothers: Albre A. Adams served in the Seabees in WWII; Jerome M. Adams served in the Army in WWII; Ramond S. Adams served in the Seabees in WWII, and I served in the Navy in WWII.

Herbert A. Adams, Rumford
Served in the Navy in WWII

I am voting in honor of my brothers: Aldaige, Ernest, Lionel, Albert, Leo Paul, and Robert Landry. Aldaige served in WWII; Ernest served 20 years, including duty in WWII and Korea; Lionel served 7 years in Korea; Albert served 20 years from 1948 – 1968; Leo Paul served 20 years from 1950 – 1970; and Robert served 4 years in the '60's.

Roland R. Landry, Springvale
Served in Korea

The McElravy brothers – John, Fred, Henry and William – all gave unselfishly in their country's service. Fred served 30 years in the Navy, including 2 tours in Vietnam. John and Henry served in the Navy in WWII, one for 3 years and the other for 7 years. William served for 22 years in the Marines, including 2 tours in Vietnam.

William McElravy, Searsport
Served 22 years in USMC from 1953–75

Left to right: Bill, Henry, John and Fred McElravy, with sister Mary Alice

I am voting in honor of the Nichols brothers; two served in the Army, one in the Navy in WWII, and another in Korea.

Donald E. Nichols, Augusta
Served in WW II, Korea, and Vietnam

Sons of Flora and Marinus Lindquist of West Enfield and later of Kennebunk, 8 of 10 **brothers** served in the military: Eric, Foster, Elwood, Rolfe Vernon, and Louis all served in the Army in WWII; Dean served in the Marines and Leon in the Navy in WWII; Raymond served in the Army in Vietnam and Korea and was present at the atomic bomb testing in Nevada.

June V. Cummings, Kennebunk
Emma J. Clark, Kennebunk

Left to right: Louis, Dean, Irving, Eric, Raymond and Robert Lindquist
Front: Foster Lindquist

Dedication to military service and commitment to country span decades and represent families' unselfish sacrifice and sense of duty, honor, and pride:

I am very proud of <u>my son</u>, Kevin Crowe, and <u>my husband</u>, Vernon Crowe, for their service to the United States. Kevin was in the Marines for 4 years and served in Desert Storm. Vernon was in the Navy for 23 years, duty that included Vietnam.

Debra Crowe, Norridgewock

On Election Day I will be voting in honor of <u>my grandson</u>, Scott A. Vetter, Jr., and <u>my son</u>, Edward H. Vetter, Jr. Scott has served 4 years in the USAF, including the Gulf Conflict. We are proud of him.

Edward H. Vetter, Jr. (1971)

In 1971 it was difficult to see our eldest son Edward go into the service of his country at a time when we were fighting a "conflict" in Vietnam, but we both felt that it was a duty for any one of our 5 children to serve their country. After all, his father had served in the Air Force during WWII and his grandfather in the Navy in WWI.

I feel there is not enough emphasis placed on our servicemen and how much they did and do for their country. Giving up time to serve anywhere in the world is something special to me.

Ruth Vetter, Eliot

Alvin Smart

Kenneth Smart

Russell Smart, Jr.

Russell Smart, Sr.

<u>My husband</u>, Russell O. Smart, Sr., was in the old Army Air Corps in Panama in the 40's and was a truck driver and mechanic for all kinds of military vehicles and drove convoys night and day. <u>My son Kenneth</u> served in the Marines in Vietnam and in the National Guard for a total of 30 years of service. <u>My son Russell Jr.</u> served 26 years in the Marines and the Air Force with duty in Vietnam. <u>My son Alvin</u> served 20 years in the Air Force, including duty in Saudi Arabia.

Vivian T. Smart, Stockton Springs

We are a true military family. <u>My great-grandfather</u>, Edward Crowley, fought in the Indian War and was in the Army with Custer. <u>My grandfathers</u>, Edward Harrington and Jesse D. Russell, both served in the Army during WWI. <u>My father</u>, Raymond Harrington, served in WWII, Korea, and Vietnam in the Army Air Corps and the Coast Guard and retired from the Coast Guard after 24 years of service. <u>My husband,</u> Joseph A. Medeiros, retired from the Army after 26 years of service. They all told great stories and have been in veterans' organizations to help preserve what they fought for – freedom.

Margaret J. Medeiros, Starks

August Johnson, Jr.

Eldon Johnson

George Johnson

My grandparents had 7 sons in the service, 5 of whom served in WWII and 2 in Korea; 5 served in the Army, 1 in the Air Force and 1 in the Marines: Guy, Glenn, Ray, Eldon, Maurice, George, and August Johnson. Guy died in Germany 2 days before the war ended.

Arnold R. Caron, Old Town
U.S. Navy Retired, served from 1943–1963 in WWII, Korea, and Vietnam

Glenn Johnson

Guy Johnson

Maurice Johnson

Ray Johnson

I am honoring all my family. I am voting in honor of my father, August (Gus) V. Turlo, who was injured in training during WWII. He could not serve overseas and was discharged with a disability that affected him his entire life. He was the father of 7 children, and 3 of us served in the military: my brother Patrick A. Turlo is USCG Ret. and my brother Timothy R. Turlo is USMC Ret. I also honor 2 uncles, Freddie J. Turlo, USCG Ret., and Alphonse Turlo, USAF in WWII.

Bill Turlo, Winslow
Served during Vietnam, Grenada, and Desert Storm
US Army (Ret.)

I will proudly vote in honor of <u>my two sons</u> and <u>one grandson</u>. My son, William F. Field, has served in the Navy since 1980, my son David A. Field served in the Navy from 1984-88, and my grandson, David C. Field, has served in the Navy since 1996.

Maxine L. Field, Ellsworth

I am voting in honor of <u>my son</u>, Jamie Martin, USAF, who has followed his parents in military service and is proud to be military.

Dora Albritton, Princeton, LA
Served in Air Force, including duty in Vietnam

Jamie Martin

I want to pay tribute to <u>my mother</u>, Alice E. Perkins, who served in the Coast Guard during WWII, and <u>my father</u>, Laurence G. Perkins, who served in the Navy during WWII and Korea, and <u>my brother</u>, Richard L. Perkins, who served in the Army during the Vietnam conflict.

Laurence G. Perkins

Kathleen D. P. Corbin, Augusta

Richard L. Perkins

I am proud of <u>my husband</u>, Elmer Dumond, and <u>our 3 sons</u>, Paul, Philip, and Bruce. My husband served during Korea and in Vietnam; he was a Ranger and Green Beret and received the Purple Heart and other medals for his service. All 3 sons served in the Gulf War. Paul retired as M/Sgt from the Army, Philip served in the Army and is out of the service now, and Bruce is still active duty USAF.

Ruth E. Dumond, Caribou

I am voting in honor of <u>my husband</u>, Harold Bourgeois, and <u>my son</u>, Robert Bourgeois. Harold served in the Navy during WWII and then joined the USAF and served until 1975. He was in Vietnam as was our son Robert, who served in the Navy. They are both deceased now.

Rowena M. Bourgeois, Eddington

I am voting in honor of <u>my father</u>, Joseph (Andre) Desrochers, and <u>his 4 brothers</u>. My father was the middle one of the 5 brothers, and all of them distinguished themselves in military service. <u>My father</u> served in the Army during WWII and is a Pearl Harbor survivor, the last surviving brother, who just passed away in October 2000. <u>My uncle</u>, Joseph (Arthur Henry) served in the Army during WWII and was assumed "missing in action" in 1944 or '45 while in movement to Europe. Another uncle Joseph (Julien) also served in the Army during WWII and passed away in 1956. A third uncle Joseph (Raymond) served in the Army and is also deceased. The fourth brother Joseph (Eugene Ernest) served in the Army during the Korean War, was a POW and received a Purple Heart. He passed in 1970.

Joseph A. Desrochers, Jr., Lewiston
Served in Air Force in Vietnam

<u>My father and I</u> represent two generations of military service. My father, Hormidas Sansoucy, served in the Army in WWII and Korea. He is nearly 85 years old now and very ill. I am proud to be one of his 7 children. I served during the Vietnam era but became disabled in 1966 protecting my country.

George Sansoucy, Biddeford
Served during Vietnam era

We represent 2 generations of military service. My father, Lt. Charles Davidson, served in the Signal Corps during WWII and Korea, and I served in the US Army Medical Corps from 1984-99.

Cynthia Davidson, D.O., Wells
Served as Captain in US Army

I am voting in honor of <u>my daughter</u>, Tina Marie Farris, who is on active duty with the U.S. Coast Guard stationed at Kodiak, Alaska.

Gary L. Crossman, Winterport
Retired, served from 1972-92

When I vote, I will pay tribute to <u>my uncle</u>, Richard Brooks Jones, who was killed in action during WWII. I also honor <u>my father</u>, Freeland Jones, who served in Company D, 399th Infantry Regiment of the 100th Division in the European Theater, and <u>our son</u>, David W. Walker, who served in the 12th Aviation Brigade at Wiesbaden Airfield in Germany.

Karen L. Walker, Veazie

I am proud of <u>my grandson</u>, WO1 James Dunn, whose duties require him to go to other countries to talk with other officers. He is scheduled for several more weeks of training. James was promoted to Warrant Officer in January 2001.

Norma C. Dunn, Poland

I am voting in honor of <u>my daughter</u>, Kimberly L. (Dunham) Planchon, who served for 10 years in the U.S. Air Force. She served two tours in South Korea, a tour in Okinawa, Japan, and at Air Force bases in the U.S.

Chester J. Dunham, Jr., Kennebunk

EPILOGUE

America launches "Operation Enduring Freedom" in response to terrorist attacks in New York, Washington D.C., and Pennsylvania

On **September 11, 2001**, our world as we knew it changed. Many feel our country has lost an element of innocence and that nothing will ever be quite the same again. The events in New York City, Washington, D.C., and Pennsylvania remind us all that we now live with uncertainty. It is difficult to comprehend or understand the circumstances that surround us, yet we search, nonetheless, for answers to questions that seem answer-less.

We cannot forget, nor will we forget, those who have lost their lives. We cannot forget, nor should we forget, the heroic efforts of fire, rescue and law enforcement workers who risked and sacrificed their lives so that others might survive.

Theirs was a sacrifice known and understood by the men and women veterans who have served this country.

We offer our prayers and support to the families that have been so devastatingly affected by this national tragedy.

The people of our great country will prevail. We will do so because there is a renewed sense of unity in our nation, the likes of which many Americans have never before seen or experienced.

In flags on cars and buildings across America and on the faces of citizens holding candlelight vigils from coast to coast, we see it: a renewed sense of patriotism, determination and commitment to a common goal and shared purpose, some of the very principles on which this country was founded.

Our responsibility is to keep those candles lit because their flames represent hope, and, as long as there is hope, there can be freedom.

Dan A. Gwadosky
Maine Secretary of State

ACKNOWLEDGEMENTS

Many people contributed to the publication of **Maine Remembers Those Who Served**. Without their generous help and expertise, this collection of responses honoring our veterans would not have been possible.

We extend our sincere gratitude to friends and colleagues who helped with this project:

Editor: Carol A. Kontos

Staff of the Secretary of State's Office

Staff of the Maine State Archives

Members of the Veterans' Coordinating Committee

Major General Joseph E. Tinkham, II
Adjutant General

Bertram E. Davis, Cumberland Center
U.S. Navy Retired

Howell Photography

Swardlick Marketing Group

MAINE MEDAL OF HONOR RECIPIENTS BY WAR

*POSTHUMOUS

AMES, ADELBERT
ANGLIN, JOHN
BELCHER, THOMAS
BIBBER, CHARLES J.
BICKFORD, JOHN F.
BLISS, ZENAS R.
BOWMAN, EDWARD R.
CHAMBERLAIN, JOSHUA L.
CHASE, JOHN F.
CLARK, CHARLES A.
DAVIS, SAMUEL W.
DUNCAN, ADAM
DUNN, WILLIAM
ESTES, LEWELLYN G.
FARLEY, WILLIAM
FERNALD, ALBERT E.
FRISBEE, JOHN B.
HANSCOM, MOSES C.

CIVIL WAR

HASKELL, FRANK W.
HAYNES, ASBURY F.
HESSELTINE, FRANCIS S.
HOWARD, OLIVER O.
HYDE, THOMAS W.
KENDRICK, THOMAS
KNOWLES, ABIATHER J.
LITTLEFIELD, GEORGE H.
MATTOCKS, JOHN
MATTOCKS, CHARLES P.
MCCULLOCK, ADAM
MCLEOD, JAMES
MERRIAM, HENRY C.
MERRILL, AUGUSTUS
MORRILL, WALTER G.
POOLE, WILLIAM B.
RICE, CHARLES
ROBERTS, OTIS O.

SEWARD, RICHARD E.
SMITH, CHARLES H. (USA)
SMITH, CHARLES H. (USN)
SMITH, JOSEPH S.
SPURLING, ANDREW B.
STERLING, JAMES E.
TAYLOR, THOMAS
THAXTER, SIDNEY W.
TOBIE, EDWARD P.
TOZIER, ANDREW J.
TRIPP, OTHNIEL
VERNEY, JAMES W.
WHEELER, HENRY W.
WHITTIER, EDWARD N.
WILLIAMS, ANTHONY
WOOD, H. CLAY
YOUNG, HORATIO N.

INDIAN CAMPAIGNS

BAILEY, JAMES E.
BOWMAN, ALONZO
*MCMASTERS, HENRY A.
SMITH, WILLIAM
TAYLOR, WILBUR N.

INTERIM PERIOD

GIDDINGS, CHARLES
ROBINSON, JOHN

SPANISH AMERICAN WAR

DOHERTY, THOMAS M.
FOSS, HERBERT L.

KOREAN CAMPAIGN (1871)

HAYDEN, CYRUS

PHILIPPINE INSURRECTION

CONDON, CLARENCE M.

WORLD WAR I

NONE

WORLD WAR II

DAHLGREN, EDWARD C.
*FOURNIER, WILLIAM G.
SCHONLAND, HERBERT E.
*WAUGH, ROBERT T.
ZEAMER JR., JAY

KOREAN CONFLICT

*GOODBLOOD, CLAIR
*LORING, CHARLES J., JR.
MILLETT, LEWIS L.

VIETNAM CONFLICT

BUKER, BRIAN L.
*MCMAHON, THOMAS J.
SKIDGEL, DONALD S.

PERSIAN GULF

NONE

SOMALIA

*GORDON, GARY I.

-Information provided by the Maine Medal of Honor Committee, October 1995

APPENDIX

Information for the collection was compiled from the following sources:

Chapter 1   The Early Wars: Historic Heroes

The Revolutionary War (1775-1783)
etext.virginia.edu/jefferson/quotations/
www.historyplace.com/unitedstates/revolution/revwar-75.htm
Maine State Archives

War of 1812 (1812-1815)
members.attcanada.ca/~htfergus/AmericanWar.html
www.multied.com/1812/declares.html
www.ohiokids.org/ohc/history/h_indian/pictures/war1812.html
www.semo.net/suburb/dlswoff/1812.html

Civil War (1861-1865)
www.historyplace.com/civilwar/battle.htm
www.cr.nps.gov/seac/histback.htm
encarta.msn.com
xroads.virginia.edu/
www.liberty1.org/gtsbrg.htm
www.curtislibrary.com/pejepscot/joshbiog.htm
Maine State Archives

Spanish American War (1898)
www.geocities.com/Heartland/Pointe/3048/TR/Trquotes.html
www.smplanet.com/imperialism/remember.html
www.nypl.org/research/chss/epo/spanexhib/page_4.html
www.smplanet.com/imperialism/splendid.html
www.spanam.simplenet.com/maine.htm
www.spanam.simplenet.com/mainparts.htm

Chapter 2   The World Wars: Sacrifices Around the Globe

World War I: "The Great War" (1914-1918)
www.umkc.edu/imc/vetsday.htm
home.iae.nl/users/robr/poppies.html
www.lib.byu.edu/~rdh/wwi/1917/wilswarm.html
kids.infoplease.lycos.com/ce6/A0862004.html

World War II: (1939-1945)
encarta.msn.com
memory.loc.gov/ammem/today/ec07.html
www.execpc.com/~dschaaf/attack.html

Background
www.afa.org.magazine/valor/0795valor.html
home.pacbell.net/fbaldie/In_Retrospect.html
www.wplwloo.lib.ia.us/sullivanbrothers.html
www.softwhale.com/history/hist-sullivans.htm
www.pathfinder.com/photo/week/0729.htm

Chapter 2   **The World Wars: Sacrifices Around the Globe (Continued)**

World War II: (1939-1945)

Pacific Theater
www.afa.org.magazine/valor/0795valor.html
home.pacbell.net/fbaldie/In_Retrospect.html
www.wplwloo.lib.ia.us/sullivanbrothers.html
www.softwhale.com/history/hist-sullivans.htm
www.pathfinder.com/photo/week/0729.htm

European Theater
www.nando.net/sproject/dday/dday2.gif
www.historyguy.com/normandy_links.html
www.army.mil/cmh-pg/BOOKS/amh/amh-22.htm
www.ukans.edu/heritage/abilene/ikedday.html

Chapter 3   **The Cold War Era: 1945-1990**

Korean Conflict (1950-1953)
www.nps.gov/kwvm/home.htm
www.kids.infoplease.lycos.com/year/1945.html
gi.grolier.com/wwii/wwii_1.html
www.nps.gov/kwvm/war/korea.htm
www.korean-war.com/chronology/KoreanWarOverview.html
korea50.army.mil/history/factsheets/medals.html
newslibrary.krmediastream.com/cgi-bin/search/me
www.pbs.org/wgbh/amex/macarthur/filmmore/reference/primary/macspeech06.htm
encarta.msn.com/

Vietnam Conflict (1961-1975)
www.pbs.org/battlefieldvietnam/timeline
www.geocities.com/pentagon
www.fas.org/dod-101/ops/vietnam.htm
www.eb.com
www.hqusareur.army.mil/htmlinks/HISTORY/TET.htm
www.vwam.com/vets/ptet/hueps.html

International Incidents
Bay of Pigs Invasion (1961)
www.la.mvla.k12.ca.us/LC/CubaPoli/cuba_4/cuba_4a.htm
encarta.msn.com/
library.thinkquest.org/11046/days/bay_of_pigs.html
www.parascope.com/articles/1296/bayofpigs.htm
www.aha.ru/~mausoleu

Cuban Missile Crisis (1962)
encarta.msn.com/

Berlin Wall (1969-1970)
encarta.msn.com/index/conciseindex/AC/0AC4C000.htm?z=1&pg=2&br=1
userpage.chemie.fu-berlin.de/BIW/wall.html
wysiwyg://133/http://kids.infoplease.lycos.com/ipka/A0107583.html

Chapter 3   **The Cold War Era: 1945-1990**

International Incidents
Grenada (1983)
www.historyguy.com/Grenada.html
www.army.mil/cmh-pg/faq/lcas.htm
www.fas.org/man/dod-101/ops/urgent_fury.htm

Lebanon (1983)
www.beirut-memorial.org/history/embassy.html
www.dssrewards.net/english/twa847.html

Panama (1988)
www.specialoperations.com/Operations/Just_Cause/Operation_profile.htm
www.bragg.army.mil/18abn/panama.htm
www.fas.org/man/dod-101/ops/just_cause.htm

Chapter 4   **Today: The World's Peacekeepers**

The Persian Gulf (1990-1991)
www.geocities.com
www.pbs.org/wgbh/pages/frontline
www.desert-storm.com
www.historyguy.com/GulfWar.html
www.va.gov/health/environ/faq.html
www.usdreams.com/Schwarzkopf.html

Somalia (1992-1994)
www.arab.net/somalia/history/so_hope.html
www.lycos.com

Haiti (1994)
kids.infoplease.lycos.com/ipka/A017612.html

Kosovo (1999-present)
www.infoplease.lycos.com/spot/kosovo
www.kosovo.mod.uk/natoforces.html
www.nato.int/docu/facts/2000/kosovo.html